ONCE MORE WE
SAW STARS

ONCE MORE
WE SAW
STARS

Jayson Greene

RANDOM HOUSE
LARGE PRINT

Excerpt of "Between the Bars," written by Steven
Paul Smith, provided by courtesy of Universal Music
Publishing Group, copyright © Universal Music-Careers,
on behalf of Itself and Spent Bullets Music.

A portion of this work originally published as "Children
Don't Always Live" in **The New York Times** Opinion
column on October 22, 2016.

Some names and identifying details have been changed to
protect the privacy of individuals.

Cover photograph taken by the author, Coney Island, 2015
Cover watercolor by iStock/Getty Images
Cover design by Jenny Carrow

The Library of Congress has established a
Cataloging-in-Publication record for this title.

ISBN: 978-1-9848-8620-0

www.penguinrandomhouse.com/large-print-format-books

FIRST LARGE PRINT EDITION

Printed in the United States of America

10 9 8 7 6 5 4 3 2 1

This Large Print edition published in accord with
the standards of the N.A.V.H.

To Greta and Harrison

To get back up to the shining
    world from there
My guide and I went into that
    hidden tunnel;
And following its path, we took
    no care
To rest, but climbed: he first, then
    I—so far,
Through a round aperture I saw
    appear
Some of the beautiful things that
    Heaven bears,
Where we came forth, and once
    more saw the stars.

—Dante Alighieri, **Inferno**

CONTENTS

One

THE ACCIDENT

HOW SHOULD WE START, SWEETIE? Maybe with one of the silly games we invented together. They meant nothing to anyone else, but everything to us. There was the time we pretended, for half an hour, that the ramp outside of a building was an elevator. You would press your finger to a brick; I would make a beeping noise. I would say "Going down!" and you would run down the ramp, laughing. That was the whole game. It was enough.

Or: We're on the beach. You are two years old. You saw the beach once before, when you were fourteen months; you did not enjoy it. The sun on your skin felt invasive (you shared your mother's aversion to direct sunlight). The sand moving beneath your feet and hands fascinated you at first but quickly unnerved you; the ground had never stuck to

you before, nor had it proven unreliable. The
sea thundered. You wound up in my arms,
squirming.

Today, you are older, and you are unafraid.
You are wearing a polka-dot red cardigan
over a striped green dress and a bright red
hat, and in your left hand is a mango on a
stick from the boardwalk vendor. I carry you
out past the Coney Island pier; I take off
my shoes and set you down with your small
shoes on. You run out, mango stick held out
carefully to your side. I walk after you.

The ocean is enormous to you, and I sense
the thrill of awe and fear little people feel when
confronted with the world's vastness. You
look up at me and I smile; I don't seem scared.
My shoes are off, I point out; would you like
to take off yours? Your eyes go thoughtful,
and then you nod. We walk up together to
the mouth of the impossible ocean. The wet
sand is cold; it's only May. Individual sand
grains twinkle. "Look, sweetie pie, a shell,"
I say, pointing to your feet. You reach down
and scoop it up out of the wet sand. It is a
fragment, something that fits between your
tiny finger and thumb. There is a clump of

sand at its point; you hold it up in my face, grinning, as I pretend to be disgusted.

"Ewww!!"

You laugh that throaty, snuffly, catching giggle of yours. The waves run closer, reaching us. For the only time in your life, you feel ocean water running over your toes.

✧

The brick fell from an eighth-story windowsill on the Upper West Side of Manhattan. Greta was sitting on a bench out front with her grandmother. The two of them were chatting about a play they had seen together the night before. It was a live-action version of the kids' show **Chuggington,** in which some talking train cars help their friend Koko get back on track after she derails.

"Koko got stuck!" Greta exclaimed over and over. The moment seemed lodged in her brain, my mother-in-law told us later. She was struck by the simplicity of the predicament, the profundity of the call for help.

Reporters interviewed the aide of the elderly woman who lived on the floor—the woman whose windowsill crumbled. Even in print, I recognized the sickened wonder in her voice, her newly dawning understanding of the malevolence and chaos of the world: "It was like an evil force reached down . . ."

✧

We left our E-ZPass in the apartment. Stacy and I realize this only upon arriving at the mouth of the tunnel en route to the Weill Cornell ER. The gate fails to lift as we approach and we almost plow through it. The man at the tollbooth tries to reckon with us, incoherent and hysterical and blocking traffic.

"Our daughter's been in a serious accident," Stacy yells to him.

He peers behind us at the empty car seat, confused. "Where is she?" he demands.

"She's with my mother!" Stacy says. Cars honk as the pressure of the line builds behind us.

"Please, she is in the hospital," I interject. "Please just let us go."

He waves us on. "Just don't get in an accident!" he calls into our window as the bar lifts.

We'd received the phone call from Stacy's mother, Susan, only twenty minutes before. "Oh, Jayson, it's so horrible," she had said—her first words. The scenario she described was still sketchy: there had been two chunks of brick; there were paramedics on the scene. Susan was in the back of a second ambulance, and Greta was in the first, already en route to the hospital. Susan had been struck as well, in the legs.

"Where is Greta?" I demanded.

"She's up ahead," Susan said. "She's breathing on her own now. They told me she's breathing on her own."

Her voice was fuzzy, disoriented, and we heard other muffled voices, paramedics demanding things of her. A male voice cut in behind her, asked Susan something sharply. I could tell from her faltering response that she was struggling to connect the dots.

"Susan, please tell me," I said, firmly and slowly. "Where did the brick hit Greta? Did it hit her in the head?" When I said the word "head," I felt something break up my voice, an elemental **thing** I wasn't familiar with yet.

"It hit her in the head, yes," Susan said. I yelled this information over my shoulder to Stacy, who screamed instinctively.

"My baby girl," she cried, sobbing convulsively.

During the eternal drive up the highway, neither Stacy nor I speak in specifics. She reaches over and grabs my palm, her voice trembling. "She has to be OK. She just has to be. There's no other option."

✧

We leave our car behind us in valet parking and run into the lobby. We reach the security guard, and I say it again, for the second time: "Our daughter's been in an accident, and she's in the ER." I watch his face soften; I am already learning what happens when you tell people this news.

"I'm sorry," he says, and waves us on.

There is a visible trail of crisis in the ER entryway, a smear on time leading all the way up the hall, and I feel us walking through it. I hear someone to my left ask, "Are these the parents?" and some part of me registers the grimness of that designation: "the parents." Up ahead, a paramedic waves to us urgently.

We follow into a corner room, maybe twelve by twelve, with a table in the middle and doctors and nurses crowding around it. In the center of it is Greta, stripped down to her diaper and pitifully tiny, her eyes closed and her mouth open. I watch as team members lift her arms and legs like she's a sock puppet. I remember seeing the upper roof of her mouth, the pearly islands of her teeth. I have no memory of the injury on her head; my mind either refuses to note it or has erased it.

There are things you see with your body, not with your eyes. Stepping away, I feel something evaporate, a quantum of my soul, perhaps, burning up on contact. I am lighter, somehow immediately less me, as if some massive drill has bored into my bones, extracting marrow. I glance at Stacy, grey and motionless in a hallway chair, and see the same life force exiting her frame. Susan is on a stretcher down another hallway, out of our sight. We wait.

I take out my phone and call my parents, on vacation in New Orleans. I try my mother's cell phone first: no answer. I leave a voice mail of some sort. I pace the length of the reception desk, try my father's cell phone. Voice mail. My brother: voice mail. I have dropped through a wormhole, it seems, or fallen into a crack in time. My unaware family and friends are living above it. On their timeline, Greta is still fine.

It is John, my brother, who finally picks up. I try to relay the seriousness of the situation, and I can tell that he does not or is refusing to grasp it.

"Oh, Jay, I'm so sorry," he says. His voice is sympathetic, the reaction to a commonplace childhood injury, a terrifying but temporary moment in any young parent's life. "My heart goes out to you, man. There's absolutely nothing worse. I remember when Ana"—his eight-year-old daughter—"was bitten by the dog. It was the worst day of my life. You feel so **powerless.**"

I try to emphasize my foreboding through the phone: "It's **bad,** John," I say.

"She's going to be OK," he tells me, and I hear a touch of a plea behind the reassurance in his voice. I don't know very much yet. But I had seen the haunted looks on the EMTs' faces when I entered, and I had already beheld the terrible sight of Greta's body, lifeless and birdlike, lying limp on a massive table.

"No, John," I say grimly. "No, I think she won't."

✧

The trauma team rushes Greta from intake into another hallway to perform a CAT scan, which will reveal the depth and severity of her head injuries. All that precious stuff in her head—what state is it in? Stacy and I are already silently calculating odds. Greta began speaking in sentences startlingly early; she was obsessed with dogs, and Stacy and I joked that we would get her one when she was old enough to tell us "I want a puppy" in a sentence. When she told us that at fourteen months, we laughed and expanded the minimum qualifications ("Mother, Father, I very much would like a dog, and I promise to help walk it and feed it"). We needed more time, we reasoned. We were sure we had it.

The CAT scan reveals a bleed in her brain, and she is rushed into emergency surgery. The bleed is so severe, apparently, that no one is dispatched to update "the parents" on her condition. After waiting an interminable-seeming amount of time in the ER, I seek out our social worker, a man whose face we had just been introduced to numbly minutes ago. He is holding a plastic bag, which he hands to Stacy: Greta's gold sandals, stained with blood. Stacy accepts the bag without reaction and lets it dangle at her side. "Where is our daughter?" I ask.

The social worker knocks on the big blue door of the CAT scan room, then tentatively pushes it open; it is empty save for one team member.

We are ushered to another floor. There we sit, waiting, texting friends and loved ones listlessly.

Our close friends Danny and Elizabeth show up, Elizabeth bearing a pendulous bag of sandwiches, in that helpless way you do when you can't show up empty-handed but have nothing to give. Stacy had texted them when we were still in triage: "Greta's been hurt and I don't know if she's going to be OK."

These two are first responders in all of their friends' lives, arriving first to a crisis with the sirens still blaring and the caution tape up. Their own lives are messy in the rumpled and continuous way of true urban bohemians, their two-bedroom apartment nearly crumbling under the weight of thousands of books and odd vintage baubles and the hundreds of art projects of their astonishingly wise five-year-old child, Clara. They were the ones showing up late to a party with hair astray and faces red, Elizabeth alluding to some jaw-droppingly unlikely set of circumstances with a wave of a hand and muttering, "Don't even ask." But when the slightest calamity befell anyone in their generous orbit, they dropped every single piece of their precarious juggling act and knelt at your side. There were only two of them, but somehow when they arrived you felt encircled. We had seen them perform this role for their innumerable friends and acquaintances and total strangers that one friend had vouched for. Now it is our turn. Elizabeth sets the sandwich bag down on the floor and hugs us both wordlessly.

Stacy's brother, Jack, and his girlfriend of nine years, Lesley, come next, their faces broken and streaming. They take their seats on either side of Stacy, who sits with her knees drawn up to her chest. I remember almost nothing from this moment, only the shape of the corner we sit in and then the dim figures of two police detectives standing near the elevators; they had arrived from the scene of the accident. The rest—how much time passes, what I say to Stacy or Jack, whether I get up to go to the bathroom, whether I text anyone the news, whether I say anything at all in particular—is a penny slipping beneath dark water.

I think about Greta, knowing that whatever of her that survives will be damaged. I imagine raising a shell of my child, a body that keeps growing while a mind flickers dimly. I think about never hearing her speak again. I think about wheelchairs, live-in care, an adult Greta prostrate and mute, occupying our spare bedroom. I think, briefly, about expenses—how would we shoulder that burden?

Eventually, the surgeon emerges. We stand up, pointlessly. He is the television-drama vision of a neurosurgeon: gaunt, grey, with hollowed eye sockets and some slight wasting at his temples. He seems to be made entirely of cartilage under his scrubs.

He lowers his bony frame into the chair next to us and clasps his hands between his knees. "I wish I had better news for you. We removed as much of her skull as we could to allow the brain to swell, but the bleed was rather severe."

I feel him choosing his words as carefully and severely as possible: our false hope is a blockage, and his job is to cut it out at the root and leave nothing behind to grow.

"So you're saying that her recovering would be sort of . . . a miracle situation?" Stacy asks.

"I would say so, yes," he answers. He looks at us, his eyes as sorrowful as his voice is laconic. He adds, more quietly, "This is one of those situations where I'd love to be wrong."

We are sent down to another wing of the hospital, waiting for nurses to stabilize Greta.

Susan is wheeled out in a hospital gown, her legs bruised and swollen and her face ashen. Her eyes are spent and wild, lost in the way I associate with patients deep in Alzheimer's: **There is something terribly wrong**, the eyes say, **but it is too large for me to figure it out.**

She breaks into sobs the second she sees us, her body folding in the chair as if our gaze were shriveling her. Stacy rushes over, kneeling down.

"It's not your fault," she says quietly to Susan. "It's not your fault."

Susan cries like a small child into her shoulder until she grows still.

We all settle in and wait. There is a fish tank to our right, separating the hallway and the bustle of the hospital from us in our misery. The bag of sandwiches sits, unloved, on the table.

"Is anyone hungry?" Elizabeth finally asks, the question emerging like a puff of breath in frozen air.

Stacy pokes at the bag disinterestedly. "Maybe? Where are these sandwiches from?" Stacy's food obsessions are so fierce and pure they sometimes disconcert even her, and their persistence in this situation makes us all chuckle slightly, despite ourselves.

"They are from Corrado, a really fancy specialty market," Elizabeth says, adding with a smile, "We chose them **very** carefully. There's dill chicken in there, and roast beef, and none of them have mayonnaise."

Stacy brightens slightly, leaning forward. She opens the bag and begins to inspect each sandwich, lifting the lids on their cartons, pincering the top slice of bread with two fingers to peek beneath at the distribution of meat to cheese, to confirm mayonnaise absence, and to hunt for the dreaded presence of raw onion. As she performs this finicky little ritual, Elizabeth starts laughing; suddenly we all are.

"Mom, do you want one of these sandwiches?" Stacy asks, giggling and gasping a little. "They really are really good."

We eat and then sit with the cartons strewn around, forgotten next to torn-open mustard packets and balled-up napkins. The silence settles back in, and as the grey haze of hours stretches on with no updates, the dread consumes us again.

We know Greta is going to die, all of us, although we haven't allowed the thought into our conscious minds yet. None of us is ready for it to maraud through our subconscious, killing and burning everything it sees. But we hear the banging at the gates. We glance around us, realizing this is the last we'll ever see of the world as we've known it. Whatever comes next will raze everything to the ground.

✧

Dr. Lee, the pediatric ICU doctor on call, comes out after three hours to retrieve us. She hits a button, the doors swish open, and we enter the PICU. This place will become our Bardo, our place of death and transition, for the next forty-eight hours. Our daughter is in a room on the left wing, but Dr. Lee guides us down the right wing instead, to a small room with a fake houseplant in the corner, and some granola bars on a coffee table surrounded by three chairs.

She sits and beholds us. Her eyes are grave, attentive, compassionate. "The unthinkable has happened to Greta," she says by way of introduction. "Her condition is stable, but the brain injury is such that she will never wake up." She waits a beat, then, more quietly, "I believe her prognosis is fatal.

"I want you to be aware," she adds more gently as we sob, "that there is a lot of swelling. You should know that before going in to see her." She sits and listens silently to the sound of our hearts splitting open in that room. Then she stands up: "Let me know when you are ready to go in."

We walk into Greta's room; we are, we now understand, greeting our dead child. Her face is yellow and glistening with IV fluid, her skull swollen and blue, with obscene steel staples running down the center. We flank the bed, each holding on to a hand.

"Hi, monkey," my wife says. "We didn't get very much time together. It wasn't enough, was it?"

The staff, gathered at the edge of the bed, watches us quietly. One of them brushes a fingertip on Stacy's wrist as she steps forward to adjust something: "You two are amazing," she murmurs, then steps back. I can feel their tenderness toward us creeping into the room as our family shifts into focus: Greta is no longer a body they have spent fruitless hours trying to stabilize. She is ours, and we are hers.

We sing her lullabies as nurses tend to tubes. I almost snap a photo of her—I am a father, after all, and there is a certain logic to it. We had documented every new phase of her life, every outfit, every new playground or walk around the block, to preserve it, and in the haze of my grief, this feels no different. A nurse gently discourages me.

My parents are boarding a plane. After five attempts, my mother had finally picked up the phone in line at the **Natchez** riverboat; she had simply said, "No," quietly and firmly, and began crying in the resigned way that you do when you sense a battle has already been lost.

I check my phone at Greta's bedside and see this: "Any updates? We're about to board."

I stare at the message, unable to let them board the plane without news or to tell them my daughter is dead over text message. I simply respond, "The news is not good."

My mother texts back, "We are profoundly sad," and then they are in the air, cut off from communication and presumably as alone in their thoughts as we now are with ours.

We sit and watch the rise and fall of Greta's lungs as the machine pumps and deflates them. In her first months of life, we had a nervous habit of checking to make sure she was still breathing. Sometimes, Stacy would pull her out of her bassinet at night to lay her on her chest, where their breathing would fall in sync.

The first time we took her outside, wrapped snug against Stacy in her baby carrier, we paused at a stoplight so Stacy could lift the flap and count breaths. A neighbor, a mother of a three- and a five-year-old, walked past: Stacy made a nervous joke, and the woman smiled in acknowledgment. "They're always breathing," she assured us.

Over the next months, we began to adjust to that reality. **She's always breathing**, we told ourselves. Slowly, the part of us that we weren't even aware we were holding taut slackened, one muscle fiber at a time.

I imagine it's the same for all new parents:

you slowly learn to believe in your child's ongoing existence. Their future begins to take shape in your mind, and you fret over particulars. Will she make friends easily at preschool? Does she run around enough? Life remains precarious, full of illnesses that swoop in and level the whole family like a field of salted crops. There are beds to tumble from, chairs to run into, small chokable toys to mind. But you no longer see death at every corner, merely challenges, an obstacle course you and your child are running, sometimes together and often at odds with each other.

By the age of two, your child is a person— she has opinions and fixed beliefs, preferences and tendencies, a group of friends and favorite foods. The three of you have inside jokes and shared understandings, and you speak in family shorthand. The part of you that used to keep calculating the odds of your child's continued existence has mostly fallen dormant. It is no longer useful to you; it was **never** useful to the child; and there is so much in front of you to do.

What happens to this sense when your child

is swiftly killed by a runaway piece of your everyday environment, at the exact moment you had given up thinking that something could take all of this away at any moment? What lesson do your nerve endings learn? Sitting at the foot of my daughter's hospital bed, I am too numb to absorb any of this. But I will, soon.

✧

Some riverlike coursing of hours slips past, in the time that is no time. Eventually, Dr. Lee calls us back into the other room to discuss next steps. "The way I see it," she says, "we could take her off of life support now. Or," and she pauses, "we could talk about organ donation." She lets those words bloom and settle. Despite the severity of her head trauma, she continues, Greta's organs have been miraculously preserved. Heart, liver, kidneys—all of them untouched, in perfect condition.

"If you decide to go that route, we will first have to go through responsiveness testing to confirm that she is brain dead," Dr. Lee says. "It is a formality," she adds, cutting off our unspoken question: **Is she?** "We have seen no signs of responsiveness from Greta, but to begin our search for recipients, we must run a series of tests to certify brain death."

Dr. Lee keeps talking for a moment, as I sit back and allow the idea to wash over me. She stands up. "I will leave you two to discuss it."

Stacy and I sit alone. In retrospect, I don't think either of us had a moment's doubt. I am the writer, the overexplainer who strains to shut up so that others can avail themselves of oxygen. But it is Stacy who finds and speaks the words we need: "I need it to mean something," she tells me. "Maybe this way, it won't be for nothing."

I nod. I do not know from what clear water source she is drawing, but I know that she has found her way directly to our truth for both of us.

We send immediately for Dr. Lee and tell her: we want to pursue organ donation. It is the only simple decision we make.

✧

Our first representative from LiveOnNY, the organization in charge of the organ donation, arrives promptly afterward. His name is James, and he hands me a folder as he introduces himself, assuring me that our selflessness is saving and changing lives. I open the folder and spot that sentence printed verbatim on the first sheet. My eyes land on a list of bullet points for dealing with grief as he talks. "Cry as often as you need," one notes. "Talk about your loved one as much or as little as you like," advises another. "There is no 'should' in grief, and everyone will have different needs." Another promotes the importance of vigorous exercise, found to aid in fighting depression. I stare at them until they're seared into my brain. They are my first set of instructions on how to breathe on this new planet.

A second representative, Maura, arrives soon after. She leads us back into the room where Dr. Lee gave us Greta's prognosis to brief us on the process. It seems crucial to everyone, during this time, that we be transported into a room, any room, to be given any sort of news—they shuffle us around the same three spaces as if it might diffuse or mitigate the pain.

When the door closes, I see with dismay that Maura's eyes are full. She places a beefy red hand on her chest. "First of all, I want you to know I'm a mother, too. My heart is breaking for you. Come here, come here," she says, motioning us to hug her.

I freeze, cornered, then lean stiffly into an unwelcome embrace. She is short and stout, and I keep my eyes fixed on the crosshatching of the little window panel over her shoulder and count backward from five until she releases me.

She administers the same hug to Stacy, then sits down across from us. Tears streak down one ruddy cheek. She seems overwhelmed, unable to find the starting point for her speech about recipients, timelines, the necessary paperwork. Stacy and I sense each other's slight disbelief: Surely she didn't treat **everyone** with dying children like this?

The organ donation process, we are learning, is a strange mix of the unspeakable and the bland. On the one hand, there is the actual subject: my daughter's internal organs,

encased safely in her little body, faltering but
still warm. On the other, there is the delicate
and tangled path the state treads to extricate
them, lawfully and one by one, so it can redis-
tribute them into the bodies of other citizens.
Even here there are still boxes to be checked
somehow, a routine series of questions to be
asked and answered.

We are ushered into **another** room—a corner conference space with a long table—to be
asked these questions. Maura shuffles papers
in front of her apologetically, then picks up
her pen and sits with it poised, slightly hesitant, over the top form. Do we want coffee?
No, we do not.

"We have to ask you these before authoriz-
ing the search for recipients," she begins, still
looking down. "I just wanna say, I'm sorry in
advance for the questions here that don't apply.
We—we still have to ask them all." She keeps
her eyes fixed squarely on the desk, flicking
pained eyes up at us only occasionally, when
the questions get particularly upsetting: "Did
the patient ever use drugs?" "Was she sexually
active?" "Was she pregnant?" No, she did not.
No, she was not. No, she was not.

"I can't believe you don't have a separate form for children," Stacy moans at one point, sinking back into her chair and rubbing her eyes. "She was **two**."

My parents arrive that evening and take their places with us. Together, we fan out like figures in a religious painting. My mother sits behind me on a windowsill. I am on the floor, my head resting on her knees in an echo of my childhood.

Susan is at the foot of Greta's bed, weeping softly. "Why couldn't it have been **me**," she asks of no one in particular.

I glance up at her, and her heartbreak is so acute it is like the sun—I can't look at it. No one answers, but I think at her: **It shouldn't have been you. It shouldn't have been Greta. It should have been no one.**

Instead of keeping track of hours, we watch the big red numbers on the tall stand as they fluctuate. They track my two-year-old's heart rate, kept steady by life support, and nurses watch the screen for worrisome spikes or dips. Tubes rain from a creaky-looking stand above her bed, feeding into her body at various points I don't care to follow. Every few minutes, one of the tubes becomes twisted or kinked, triggering a dull repetitive beeping from the machine; a nurse will appear, do an irritable dance of tugging, adjusting, and jiggling, until the kink loosens and the machine falls silent.

Stacy and I take turns sleeping at the foot of her bed. There are no dreams in trauma sleep: exhaustion and shock are reliable copilots, seizing the controls when you most need them. Occasionally I repeat, out loud and with no apparent awareness of anyone listening, "I should just die. Why can't I just die?" I can feel my heart gazing up at me quizzically, asking me in between beats, **Are you sure you want me to keep doing this?** I lie down on the windowsill, telling my mother I do not know how to live.

"You had better not do anything stupid," she responds gently.

I wander around the wing in my socks for the better part of the night, making twenty or thirty trips to the bathroom, sometimes only to pointlessly wash my hands and return to my daughter's bedside. I hear my own howls of grief in the bathroom, the grey tiling covering the floor and the walls like a hyperbaric chamber, and think they must belong to someone else. I avoid my gaze in the mirror; I have no interest in learning what it feels like to meet my eyes.

No matter where I walk, I see empty hallways—no one in the waiting rooms, no other planned surgeries, no one in sight. This first night is the beginning of my reeducation: Earth is now an alien planet, and I am a visitor treading its surface. I learn tiny new skills in this time, social graces I already intuit I will need. I graciously, passively accept the hug and words of a night nurse, her eyes welling with kindness, who urges me not to "give up" on our baby. The Lord Jesus, after all, works miracles.

The setting is eerily reminiscent of Greta's birth, my wife and I huddled around her in the middle of Manhattan, gazing out windows at the city around us in an uncommon quiet. The only other humans in this alternate dimension, both times, were a handful of helpers, who seemed to have been sent specifically to usher us through the transition. On her birthday, it was Rita the midwife, Narchi the doula; on this day, it is the neurosurgeon, Dr. Lee, the PICU nurses, and the team working at LiveOnNY.

In the morning I shower in the bathroom, changing into a pair of track pants and a T-shirt my mother has bought me from a nearby Gap. My brother arrives, haggard from a red-eye flight from Colorado. Liz, Stacy's childhood best friend and sister in all but name, arrives from London. Stacy, delirious from exhaustion and trauma, murmurs instinctively, "How was your flight?"

Liz looks at her and begins laughing, her voice reassuringly vinegary through tears. "It was awesome, Stace," she says wryly. "Just great."

We catch everyone up as best we can. The doctors will arrive in a few hours to declare Greta brain dead. They will disconnect her briefly from the ventilator, monitoring closely for any signs of independent respiratory movement. They will test her brain stem reflexes, the kind that register life at its most primitive. We emphasize, dully, that they do not expect to find anything.

Because Stacy was still breastfeeding at

the time of the accident, someone apparently needs to draw her blood. Why do they need her blood? We aren't entirely sure, but it seems logical enough on some deeper plane of my brain—blood, mother's milk, eye of newt, hair of child. We are in the realm of the unholy, the bodily sacrament, and nothing surprises me. If someone had approached me and soberly explained they needed to cut out my tongue to send to the lab for samples, I probably would have opened my mouth without complaint or question.

For some reason, the blood has to be sent to Philadelphia—about three hours by van. "We'll get it there as fast as we possibly can," we are assured. Then, and only then, will the phone calls to possible recipients begin. During all of this, Greta will be kept functioning. Stacy climbs into bed with her, laying her head next to Greta's on the pillow. I place my head lightly on her chest and feel it rise and fall. There is something horrible and precious about our time together now—its limits are so clear and plain. At some point in the next twenty-four hours, we won't even have her like this.

We have been told that a nurse will be in for Stacy's blood around eight a.m., but when the hour comes and goes with no nurse and no updates, I begin to feel something unwelcome: old-fashioned irritability, a hot tingling feeling piercing the cool cavernous numbness of trauma, trickling in at the edges. My forehead tightens.

"Where are they?" Stacy moans.

"I'm sure they're coming soon," my mother says, sounding unconvinced but knowing her lines for the tense moment. The situation feels grimly familiar: a typical New York City situation where everyone sits around waiting for some pointless confusion to clear.

A nurse finally arrives with syringes and empty vials, and I sigh gratefully. As the vials fill, I pull out my phone. I am confronted by a text from a work friend: "I just heard. Please let me know if there's anything I can do for you guys, and my thoughts are with you."

"Thanks. How did you know?" I write back.

"A NY Post article."

I shift on the windowsill and look around the room. The first reporter's phone call had come the previous evening, a voice mail on

Stacy's phone. We were vaguely aware of news vans on the scene of Greta's accident, but it hasn't occurred to me yet that our story might continue to be—that **we** might continue being—newsworthy.

Susan pulls up the **Post** story, although I can't look at it. "They said I was eighty years old!" she cries, indignant. She turned sixty last week.

Forty-five minutes later, the **New York Daily News** publishes its story. This time, I look: there is a photo of my daughter, her forehead strapped to a stretcher, its wheels perched on the lip of the ambulance. The stretcher is for an adult body, and she looks tiny, toylike, in the center of it. The picture has no effect on me; sitting in front of her, I simply register it as the precursor to the nightmare we are living now. There is a photo of Susan, a police officer holding her at each elbow, the camera catching uncomprehending eyes. There is a quote from one of her neighbors, anonymous: "This is a tragedy beyond belief. This is her only grandchild."

I take my mother for a walk to the café downstairs. We are both restless souls, my mother and I, and we need some relief. I order a steam-flattened egg-and-cheese croissant and a cup of weak, bitter coffee with a red plastic stirrer. I place the croissant in the middle of the unfolded wrapper and pick the melted corners of the cheese off the edges. I wonder aloud what I will do after she is truly gone, once her body has been opened up, once we are out of the hospital without her.

There were days when I would drop off Greta at daycare and feel myself glance longingly down the little hallway into the playroom; some part of me wanted to squat on the floor with her little friends all day, to abscond from the world of adults. Maybe I can volunteer at a co-op preschool for a while. Something to help fill the hole. I sip my coffee and feel the hollow of my stomach contract as it hits bottom.

My mother goes back upstairs without me, and I venture outside to the courtyard, gazing up at a stale grey sky. It's May, but there are clouds and a damp chill in the air that hasn't burned off yet. I call my dear friend Anna, a dancer who left the city for Ohio. She recounts to me later that I tell her, "We are going to have to find friends with dead children." I have no recollection of uttering those words, but hearing them again months later it strikes me: even then, some small part of me was making long-term plans for survival.

I call my therapist, a grave and serious woman with whom I had only recently begun sessions. **She is suddenly in the deep end,** I think. I tell her what has happened, and she tells me calmly to check in with her every half an hour or hour, to keep moving. She tells me how deeply sorry she is, but her voice is emotionless, toneless. I sense her flattening her reaction, transforming herself into an inanimate object I can lean against. I sag gratefully into her weight.

When I return to Greta's bedside, the atmosphere in the room is tense: Stacy's blood vials, drawn more than an hour ago, are still sitting neglected on a nearby table. Which means they are not en route to Philadelphia, which means Greta has been stranded in twilight for hours for nothing. As I look at the vials, rage boils in me. Little failures of bureaucracy are intolerable; one of them has just crushed my daughter's skull. I go striding through the PICU, looking to hook the gaze of the first person who will meet my eyes. As it often does in hospitals, my agitation spends itself on a nurse with no control over our situation.

"I promise I'll see what I can do," she says.

A few minutes later, James reappears, nurses flanking him and hastily gathering up the vials.

"Why didn't anyone come in to take these?" Stacy demands. "This is a long process already, and we're all waiting. Greta's waiting. This is the only thing we're waiting on!"

James seems slightly bumbling and agitated, the sort of person who has been told by his superiors he needs to be more tactful with patients. His voice rises unnaturally, his eyes darting away from ours: "Look, she was going to come in," he says suddenly, "but the nurse was just really afraid that you were going to back out."

We stare at him, certain he will realize this was probably the wrong thing to say. He turns and shuffles out without apologizing. Stacy looks at me in disbelief as the door closes, and we both laugh weakly. Nonetheless, the vials have been taken. I relax slightly. I check my phone again to see an email from a reporter has arrived.

"I want to offer our most heartfelt condolences from everyone here," the man writes. "Greta looked like a magical little child. We are working on a story about her passing, and if you had anything you wanted to share, I just wanted to let you know we are here for you."

I scroll down my inbox; emails with the subject "Greta" are coming in from strangers, **Inside Edition,** WABC.

A senior administrator from the hospital comes in shortly afterward. "First off, no one knows you are here," she assures us. "But the hospital is getting blanketed with calls from reporters. Many of them are not identifying themselves or are trying to pass themselves off as family. They're calling every hospital in the city. When you are ready to leave, we will escort you out and make sure you have a discreet exit. There might be media lurking outside, and we will be watching for television trucks."

I think of news trucks crawling beetle-like up and down the city and parking outside of hospitals, hoping to get lucky with a shot of the grief-stricken parents. I am briefly overwhelmed by nausea.

The family holds a brief conference in the empty bed next to Greta's.

"OK, we need to be ready for the possibility that we will run into a reporter outside," I say. "What are we going to do?"

"If anyone asks me anything, I will give him the old Sean Penn," my brother mutters.

I wheel on him, suddenly in control of something I understand. "No, you will not. If they ask you anything, I am telling you exactly what you are going to do: you are going to say 'no comment' to them, and then you are going to walk away. The only thing they want is a story, and the first thing you do or say that isn't 'no comment' hands it to them. Do you understand?"

My brother shifts; he is the alpha, unaccustomed to being yelled at in front of others. He mutters assent. Energized, I move on to my parents to make sure they understand. I have been handed a solvable problem. Greta will not wake up, but I can keep the press at bay.

At noon, doctors arrive to administer brain death testing. I watch them crowd around her, bustling. They disconnect the ventilator, monitoring Greta's chest for independent movement. Stacy and I watch her rib cage with a terrible silent focus. She lies still, stiller than I have ever seen her. As the endless minute stretches, I become aware of burning in my chest; I am holding my own breath. Finally, they plug her back in. Her chest swells; I exhale. I do not care what is making her lungs move anymore, I simply need to see them moving.

They circle to the head of the bed to shine a light in her pupils. We stand in front of the bed and watch; we need to see those eyes again. Her lids have swollen shut, and the team has to pry them open with some effort. When the pin light hits her cornea, nothing happens—it is like light hitting a marble. My daughter's deep, soft eyes are eyeballs now; there is nothing in them.

The whole merciless process takes about fifteen minutes. I can sense the finality before the doctors actually step back and begin wrapping things up. Greta's death is legal now, clinical. She is dead in the eyes of the state.

After they leave, Stacy crawls back into bed next to Greta. We know for sure that whatever is inside Greta will never come back, and deep inside our foxhole, there is something so ghastly that it could never be called "relief"— but we experience a small letting go, a tether we can let slip into the water. We will never be asked to choose for her, never be forced to make infernal calculations about her "quality of life." She is firmly on the other side, the control wrenched from our hands.

Stepping into the hallway, I confess quietly to my brother that I am deeply worried I will lose Stacy, too. This is the sort of blow, after all, that dissolves the strongest marriages.

When I walk back in, Stacy looks up from the bedside and smiles at me. "There you are," she says, and she stands up to give me a hug and a kiss. I go for another cafeteria run, getting coffee and snack orders for everyone gathered around. As I leave the room again, she says, "I love you."

As I take the elevator down to the bottom floor, I have an impossible thought: **We are going to be OK. We will survive this. We are about to enter the unimaginable, but we are also going to pass through.** The thought lasts seconds; it is like a fish in a murky river. But I hold on to it: that kiss and that smile and that casual "I love you" saved me.

✧

When I first saw that smile, eight years earlier, I had felt a tinge of something: something in its openness and generosity, its clarity, like the world was a country highway that needed lighting.

This is exactly the sort of revisionist tall tale that parents love to regale their children with: "The first time I saw your mother, I **knew.**" Occasionally I would roll my eyes at my uncle Ricky, earnestly proclaiming for the hundredth time that his wife of fifty years, Thea, was his **bashert,** or his destined soul mate.

My own parents had no such yarn: their courtship was refreshingly flawed. On their first date, my father unwittingly brought my mother to a gay bar. ("Everyone in here is staring at you, aren't they?" he asked her, to which my mother, fighting back a smile, replied, "No, I think they're staring at **you.**") When he proposed to her fifteen months later, my mother accepted, and then my father turned whitish green and didn't speak for days. My mother, laughing, told him they didn't need to get married—she'd already done that. It wasn't until she heard him accept a job across the state on the phone a week later that he stuck his head through the doorway: "You'll still marry me, right?"

Raised at a dinner table at which these stories were laughingly retold over the years, I never had much patience for the soul mate, for the **bashert.** As far as I could tell, people found others whose lives fit with theirs, for one reason or another, and they decided to strap in to face it all together, or they didn't.

Lots of reasons played into the decision, some practical, some not, and if you decided years later that the person you chose was your soul mate? Great. Just because you landed when you jumped didn't mean you knew where you were going.

And yet. As Stacy's hand clasped mine in introduction, a new coworker standing over me at my desk, I can still remember the feeling of the information coursing from that point of contact to my brain, sending a distinct message: **This is important; pay attention.** I would dismiss it as retroactive nostalgia if the sensation didn't remain so palpable to me, the quicksilver flutter that felt eerily like recognition. Maybe this is the punishment for people who fancy themselves skeptics: they are strong-armed into believing.

We learned more about each other a month later, the first two in line for cheese cubes at our desperately bad office party, hoping food would smother our discomfort. Both of us were drifting through the latter half of our twenties: Stacy was a cellist who had fallen out of love with her instrument after graduating from conservatory, and she had arrived at this sleepy classical-music nonprofit still searching for a new purpose. I had aspirations to be a music journalist, nursing vague visions of scribbling notes over spilled beer at rock shows, and instead I found myself among silver-haired Upper West Siders at Mahler and Stravinsky concerts. Together, we carried about thirty extra pounds, and we both had bad haircuts. We leaned into each other like we were sharing a private joke.

Later we drifted toward two colleagues, who were talking about the composer Jean Sibelius (that is how bad the party was). "To me, his music is like meaningless sex," Stacy said thoughtfully, prefacing the joke with "We're at the office party, so I think this is OK." The man next to me suddenly belly-laughed, his grip on his plastic cup loosening and his shoulders softening. Everyone in the immediate vicinity became more relaxed, though they didn't notice why. I noticed.

"You have a very open personality," Stacy told me on our fourth date, a compliment I had never received, or at least one I'd never received quite like this. She said it warmly, gazing straight into my eyes. She left the rest unsaid, but I heard it clearly in her face: **And I think I love you for it.**

Everything else—the first time we spent the night together, the first trip to my parents' house for Christmas (we were busted smoking pot in the basement, for the first and only time in my life), the first dinner cooked together, my proposal eighteen months later—felt like an unfurling I saw clearly from that moment.

✧

We are facing an implacable deadline. Greta's blood pressure, currently stable, will remain so only for a finite amount of time. The team at LiveOnNY occupies a closet-sized office, manning phones and working quickly down the list of potential recipients. The hours tick by as they zero in on candidates, one by one.

Late that evening, Cynthia, a black woman with close-cropped hair, comes in to announce the results to us. There is a three-year-old boy in Philadelphia who needs a heart. There is a six-year-old girl who needs a liver. There are two grown men who are in need of a kidney.

But first Greta has to stay stable. She has

now been on life support for twenty-four hours; she will need to make it another eighteen. Looking at her little body, so profoundly compromised, I feel a sense that we are holding her here; she has someplace else to be, and she is just waiting. Like the recipients at LiveOnNY, like the families on that list: we all just have to wait.

In the middle of that night, Greta's monitor starts beeping in a new register: incessant, ominous. Her blood pressure is spiking. Nurses come in and adjust the medications in her drip, and we watch the number: down, then up, then up, up, up, past the level where her organs will remain viable for long. The ship is capsizing; we are all going down. I pace the tiny room, fall to my knees, ball my fists against the floor, and scream.

"Stay calm, Jay," my mother says.

"What more do you want from me?" I cry out, still prostrate.

Stacy strokes Greta's head as the machine beeps, whispering, "Just a little longer, monkey."

Unable to take it, I wheel out of the room and pound on the door where the LiveOnNY members are working. I open the door and regard the bleary-eyed assemblage: four people in scrubs working the world's bleakest all-night telethon. It is three in the morning.

"My daughter's blood pressure is spiking, and they are having trouble controlling it," I say with grim calm. "I need you to tell me when the surgery is going to happen. What are you doing to expedite this? My daughter has been through too much already."

Cynthia gestures hopelessly toward her phone: "We are flying everyone into place. Right now, I am hoping the surgery will be at eight a.m., but there is a chance it could be at ten a.m. or somewhat later."

Somewhat later? Standing in the doorway, I think of my daughter's ruined body, her chest rising and falling by the grace of equipment. I think about her soul, trapped in between stages like a fly hitting a glass window. Then I say something terrible. I look Cynthia in the eye and say, "If she doesn't make it, the pointlessness of this will haunt me forever."

I watch this woman—who has spent the last twelve hours trying to save the lives of multiple families across the country, who has been juggling a number of gruesome and unimaginable factors in her head for hours—collapse. Her shoulders sag, and she moans involuntarily, "Don't, please." I turn and leave, the door closing just as her forehead touches the desk.

When I return to the room, Greta's blood pressure has dipped down a bit. It holds for a moment underneath the ceiling of alarm. My mother and Stacy and I hold ourselves and wait. It ticks down another notch.

"There you go," my mother whispers. "There you go."

Greta is inside somewhere; she is holding on.

Stacy kisses the staples on her head. "You're doing such a good job, monkey."

Huddled over my family, I look out the window to the glimmering buildings crowding out the sky. The thought flashes once like a pinprick on my consciousness: **The city killed her.** We did this. Stacy and I, alone in our families, were foolish enough to attempt to rear a baby in the heart of this crowded and clamorous place.

✦

My mother lived in New York for years as a nurse in her early twenties. When I was a kid, I listened to her hero stories about dancing on Avenue C in the 1970s, walking down back alleys stagger-drunk in the middle of the night and surviving by the grace of God. But she left, and by the time she had children, she was hours north and light-years away from the city's perpetual chaos. My father had grown up miserable and trapped on Long Island, seeing the city as a pocked, broken place that reflected the worst human nature had to offer. My brother and his wife had met in New York, lived through the then-hottest summer on record in a fourth-floor walk-up in pre-gentrification Williamsburg, and then abruptly quit their jobs and moved to Colorado, instantly shedding ten pounds and a constant sense of grievance in the process. Their first son was born four years later.

But Stacy and I had embraced the hot city, set up our tent, and lit our hearth fire there. As a baby, Greta slept through the eruption of car alarms, through scattered shouts from open windows down the block, through the occasional yowling of stray cats. We treated the city's dangers as a loud roaring noise that was always just around the corner. Our neighbor got mugged; we didn't. Our car window was smashed; nothing was taken.

We had been foolish and hubristic and reckless, and we had paid the ultimate price.

✧

The sun is above us, announcing the day and everything it brings. We gather around Greta as a family: my brother, Danny and Elizabeth, my parents, Susan. Stacy's brother, Jack, has just returned from an awful errand back to our apartment; he'd walked into her still-full bedroom, spilling over with the physical facts of her life, and grabbed Greta's favorite stuffed animal, Daisy, a yellow dog named after my mother's golden Lab, and her blanket, with ducks on it, that had been Stacy's as a baby. He's also brought Greta's scarlet dress with polka dots, the one she would request by name as "my pretty dress." She took visible pleasure in the way it fanned out over her legs when she walked in it, and once we caught her, in front of her little toy mirror, shyly swishing it with her hands.

Along with all of this, Jack grabbed his guitar, and he sits now and begins playing. We lay Greta's pretty dress over her body, tuck Daisy under her arm, and cover her with the duck blanket. We are in a moment of respite, and it feels momentarily like a family gathering.

The time of the surgery approaches. I feel a panicked foreboding, a desperate need for the door to stay closed. My daughter is still here in front of me, breathing and intact. The details and particulars of how and why suddenly don't matter to me when confronted by the thought of her sudden total absence. **Keep her here,** I think.

Nurses knock, and a wild roaring goes up in my ears—blood is pounding, and I am receiving the most primal signal in all of evolution. **Don't let them take her.**

I look around and see my brother weeping openly, his face crumpled, a sight I have seen maybe once before in my life. I stand up, surrounded by them, and suddenly feel as if I've stepped onto a stage. This is my Greek tragedy, and the conclusion relies on me.

"Hey there, baby girl, you did such a good job," I say in a voice of bright cheer. "It's time to go now, OK? I'm going to walk with you every step of the way, OK?"

Nurses flank her bed, gathering up the tubes to move her. I feel watery, as if my vision were suddenly going to go. I straighten. **This is going to feel like it is going to kill me,** I think, reasonably. **But all I have to do is step into it, right now. And then I will not die.**

I lift a foot, feel the blood drain from my head, place one hand on the back of her bed as they begin to wheel her out. I think of the biblical figure Nahshon, appointed by Moses, wandering head-deep into the Red Sea. The quiet sobbing in the room breaks into howls. I remain silent. I am looking at the top of her head, bluish from the last forty-eight hours but still bird's-egg beautiful and fragile. We are halfway down the hallway to the doors; the world as it will soon be, a world without Greta in it, lies on the other side.

The nurse to the right pushes the button and the doors swish open. We maneuver the bed at an angle and around the corner, then to the elevator.

"Just a little further, monkey," Stacy whispers.

I look at my broken daughter's body. She has done such an incredible job. I well up with an immense and ghastly pride at her last demonstration of will and determination.

The elevator descends. I start shuddering, bodily. **This is going to feel like it's going to kill me, but all I have to do is step into it, and it won't.** I look down at Greta's hands, her small fingers curled at the edges of the duck blanket the way they would when she was asleep. The doors open. I feel it again, that medieval urge. One is not meant to surrender the body of one's child. But we are here, and there is no more time. I take my hand off the rail and the bed with my daughter on it moves on. Greta is gone.

Stacy and I collapse into each other's arms, feeling the empty space already between us that we will never be able to fill. Some part of us, I believe, is still down there, clutching on to each other and wondering how and why we didn't die.

When I come back to the room, there is a palpable sense of relief, one that no one would have vocalized. The pieces of our lives are scattered everywhere, and we can never pick them up again; there is some peace in immediately understanding that. When a tree caves in the side of your house, you laugh quietly to yourself in wonder at the damage and its irreversibility: there's no way anyone expects us to pick **that** up. Our role as crucial actors in Greta's death is over. Now it is time to mobilize for many other things: for phone calls, for a service, for the world.

I look out at the buildings again, and the terrible sense of prophecy I felt earlier is gone. Death visits all corners of the world: it comes for drunk teenagers who careen off dark country roads; it comes for babies tangled in Venetian blinds in tract homes; it comes for children found floating in suburban pools. These are just buildings; they have no special role to play.

Two

THE AFTERMATH

IT IS AUGUST, NINE MONTHS BEFORE the accident; you are sixteen months old. We are renovating our kitchen, and the apartment is an unlivable mess. I am taking you to see Susan for the day, who has been watching you more often as the renovation drags on. Our lives are chaotic, exhausting, unmanageable, safe.

"Time to go, baby girl!" I call.

You are sitting ten feet away on the rubber mats covering the concrete in our tot lot. You rub idly at your side with a broken piece of sidewalk chalk, leaving a pink smudge. You say nothing.

I place the half-eaten banana I have been holding in my left hand on the stroller canopy, next to the balled-up piece of string cheese, and squat beside you. "We're going to go see Grandma Suz," I remind you.

"Yeah, we're gonna go see **Gam**-ma Suz,"

you agree, not looking up. "Grandma Suz" is a single three-syllable word in your voice, with the accent on "Grand," an offbeat triplet with a falling melody.

"But we gotta go if we're going to see Grandma Suz, honey," I say again, "so you've got to get in your stroller."

You stand up: "No, I don't wanna get in my stroller," you declare, and waddle off.

It is 8:00 a.m. on a Saturday, and you and I have been together for three hours. You yelled at us from your crib starting at 4:30. Our bedroom is a living room pretending to be a bedroom, with French doors splitting it in half, and your voice pierces straight through them. You haven't slept past 5:00 a.m. in months, and in desperation, we have unplugged the baby monitor.

By the time I surrender, you have been calling our names for twenty minutes or so, and your voice has turned peevish: "MOMMY-DADD-YYYYY!!!" I sit up, pausing for a moment for a quick sensory inventory: my head feels viscous and the floor feels too far away. Groaning, I stand.

I close the bedroom door behind me, brushing the plastic curtain in the doorway from my face, and walk through our upturned living room. To my left, a circular saw sits atop our disgorged air-conditioning unit, which has faded from white to grey to blue-black under successive layers of dust. I slip on the flip-flops outside the bedroom to keep my feet clean, grit crunching as I walk. I round the hall to your bedroom door, sidestepping a Tupperware bin of dirty dishes. We have running water again now, but still no kitchen sink, so we pile our used dishes in the bin each night and float them in our bathtub. The two bedrooms, ours and yours, are the only ones with bare floors, which we wipe down every day, a losing battle against entropy.

I open your door. You are standing up on your mattress in your crib, your hands on the edge, your legs swaying beneath you. You're like a shipwreck survivor in the room filled with our clutter. "I want up," you announce.

I choose my path to you carefully, winding around living room chairs, my violin, Mommy's neglected cello in its big red case. I reach down into the crib as you reach up, and we connect at my hip in one smooth motion.

"I want Mommy milk," you say.

Together, we pick our way back through the apartment, you hugging me close, gazing around with mild interest at the disaster we have made of your home. I deposit you feet-first on the bed.

"Hi, sweetie," Mommy coos at you, her eyes still closed. Pale sun hints down on the rooftops outside our window. You stand up and regard them for a moment, your hands on our headboard.

"Look, Greta, you can see the moon," I say, pointing.

You agree and then flop down. Mommy lifts her shirt and pulls you in close; you nurse, squirming the whole time and kicking your legs with pleasure and excitement. Lying next to you, your little feet thudding against my shoulder, I taste accumulated exhaustion in the back of my throat.

"You smell tired," Stacy would say in those days when I would come in to kiss her; apparently, after a certain threshold, I began to exude it like rot.

You finish nursing and push backward off the bed, scooting your way to the floor butt-first. It is my morning to get up with you, so I scoop you up the second your bare feet touch the floor. We get dressed and leave together, talking in low tones. We are letting Mommy sleep; we will see Mommy later; we are going to the playground. The playground is outside; we put shoes on for outside; which shoes do we want to put on? We are putting on our pink shoes; let me help you with those. OK, you can do it yourself. OK, let me help you.

On the playground, I watch you try to climb the monkey bars. Your foot keeps missing the lowest bar. I'm watching for the right moment, between tired and overtired, to begin our journey; it's like trying to isolate a hue of pink in a sunset. I text Susan, "Looks like we're getting on the train in twenty minutes," rounding down optimistically. I call to you again: "Hey, baby girl, maybe if you get in the stroller you can eat your banana?"

You concede. I strap you in and we leave the tot lot just as other children start to show up, trailed by bleary-eyed parents. My phone tells me there is a train arriving in seven minutes. I swipe my card, nodding to the attendant.

She hits the buzzer to unlock the emergency door and I push you through. The whole door-buzzing thing is a charade, since the door is always unlocked anyway.

This platform was closed for nearly a year after you were born, so you didn't see the subway much. When it reopened, it looked exactly the same: "They just removed the asbestos," joked Stacy. Overhead, rutting pigeons coo in the rafters. I glance down the track and spot the lights of the B train, one station away, its headlights glowing. I don't say anything to you, as you are nearly asleep. I have timed our journey impeccably.

As the train pulls up and the doors shudder open, I text "On schedule" to Susan. I push your stroller over the lip of the entrance, lock the wheels, and sink into an empty seat. We have a long journey ahead of us. I will lift your stroller up by the base, straining and grunting up crowded flights of steps; I will wedge your front wheels in between two closing subway doors. We will race heedlessly down the cream-colored sidewalks of the Upper West Side when we emerge, an hour later, aboveground into the morning light. I will retrieve you, laughing, from Susan's the next day. The city we move through is still a welcoming one, and we hurtle through it, oblivious and invincible.

✧

One hour after we surrender Greta's body to surgery, hospital administrators arrive to sneak us into the parking lot. We huddle near the exit in the disorienting sunlight while they scan the perimeter: no news trucks.

We find ourselves saying good-bye to Susan, who chooses to go home—straight back to the apartment in which Greta spent her last night, around the corner from the accident, bits of her last breakfast still on the high chair. "I'll be fine," she says dismissively.

I glance wildly at Jack and Stacy, feeling lost: Surely this is a terrible idea? And someone will say so? But Jack and Stacy relent: they have a long history of failing to persuade her to see things their way. I watch her lower herself painfully into a car with her injured legs and the door shuts, swallowing her. I want to chase after her, to scream at everyone that we need to save her from herself, but instead I just stand there.

Jack retrieves our car and we pull into traffic, suddenly enveloped again by the city. I sit shotgun, Liz and John and Stacy in the back. Someone discovers a carton of sliced watermelon rotting beneath the front seat, and the smell is overpowering. "That's awful," Jack croaks, sputtering, while Stacy laughs in the backseat, swiping in front of her face as her eyes water. The odor is a reminder of the genial mess that has recently been our lives. We roll the windows down to let in air, and Jack blasts music.

There is a cleaning lady in our apartment right now—an appointment we forgot to cancel. She knows about the accident. I try to imagine, dimly, what it must be like for her, scrubbing the counters with milk-stained baby cups on it, knowing that the child who gripped them days earlier is dead.

To kill time, and to put off facing our home, we converge on Jack and Lesley's studio apartment in Park Slope. We unlock the dog gates containing their pit bulls, Lia and Ivan, and collapse in their living room. Stacy lies on the couch with Liz, and the two of them fall asleep. Drained of color, they resemble still lives.

I bend over Jack's stereo and transfer the music from the car: "I know there's gonna be good times," croaks a sampled voice. Beers are opened. We move into the small, chain-linked backyard, pull up the old green lawn chairs sitting on wood chips. Ivy crawls up the brick wall above us.

We find ourselves momentarily buoyed by a strange survivors' cheer, telling family stories and laughing. Some are even hospital stories, small absurdities that arose from the fog and confusion of grief. Only the mention of Susan punctures the surface: we all go quiet, and our fragile bubble pops. Suddenly our ugly bruising rises to the surface, and we see ourselves for who we are: a broken family, huddling together for warmth and still bleeding. Then someone tells a joke, and just as smoothly the bubble re-forms.

I learn very quickly about the bubble and how it works. There is a quicksilver fluidity to extreme tragedy, one you adapt to intuitively. It's an operation that requires only your nerve endings and your immediate chemical needs for survival. Every single fluid in your body is pumping overtime—adrenaline, endorphins, blood. It's like a river that grows wild in storm time.

As the afternoon light fades, our backyard party dies down. Jack hooks empty beer bottles with his fingers, grabs the grease-stained paper plate with its remaining bite of sandwich, and pushes open the screen door. Lesley's dog Ivan gallops inside and leaps for the couch. Stacy kneels down to hug Lia, who jumps up and places her paws on Stacy's shoulders, kissing her face in the frantic way dogs do when they sense distress.

"I know, Lia," Stacy murmurs, turning her face to escape the uncomfortable intimacy of a direct dog-to-mouth kiss. "You are a sweet one. You can tell everybody's sad, can't you?"

We cram back into our car, a baby-blue Honda Fit with chipped bumpers that now sports a fresh parking ticket slipped beneath the wiper. I sit up front again, while Stacy drives and my mother and father cram in the back. Jack has quietly uninstalled the car seat.

We've been warned by neighbors that the

press has been stalking our building. A **New York Post** reporter has been spotted sauntering up and down the block, a microphone concealed in a piece of newspaper. The thought of a microphone jabbed in my face is sickening, so I pull out my phone and start drafting a statement in case we are cornered, while Stacy and my parents make small talk.

I have cultivated the habit of distracted writing like this the way my father, a urologist, had learned to bolt upright in the middle of the night when his pager beeped. I am a music journalist and editor, and I've spent years writing in every crevice of life I can find: standing up on the subway holding an iPad, muttering voice dictation while walking to the corner for milk.

This manic behavior is partly my nature, but I'm also fighting against an original-sin sense of guilt: I have chosen a foolhardy profession, far from my inherited notions of what "hard work" looks like. My mother and father worked in the medical field, and each had painstakingly climbed a few socioeconomic class rungs to do it.

My mother's family was Irish, working

class, from the red Republican belt of western New York. Her parents expected her to marry a local boy when she was seventeen. She left for nursing school instead, worked night shifts, married her first husband, had my brother, discovered the man she had married was an alcoholic, emptied all his bottles in the garbage, and left to be a single mother. When she met my father, she had already coolly determined that if she had to go it alone for the rest of her life, she could.

My father grew up the youngest of a splintered and unhappy Long Island family, yearning to escape. When he didn't get into the medical schools he wanted in the States, he applied to the University of Bologna, in Italy; it accepted him. Without speaking a word of the language, he gulped, boarded a plane, and began a three-week immersion course in Italian before beginning anatomy and premed courses—entirely in Italian.

I didn't have a gritty origin story. I was the beneficiary, encouraged and indulged, shuttled and safeguarded. I was a milk calf, my muscles too tender and my skin too soft, and I had chosen an absurd career path, with prospects somewhere between small-town golf pro and birthday-party magician. I had used up my indulgences.

So I invented my writing time. I wrote with Greta strapped into a BabyBjörn, feeling the rise and fall of her breath on my chest. This combination of the two vocations, the painstaking way I made them slot together at neat angles—I was a father, I was a writer—soothed my suspicions that my life was a summer-camp version of other people's.

As we park, I finish the statement. It is brief, a paragraph, a simple plea to be left alone. Satisfied, I tuck my phone away. I've found something else my writing can do: protect my wrecked little family.

We round the corner to face a blessedly empty street, and I exhale. I ignore the sidewalk chalk on the stoop beneath my feet spelling out Greta's name—a play session from five days ago. There is a sign taped to the front door fending off the press, put up by one of our neighbors. Behind it, our porter, Jose, is spraying Windex. He speaks very little English; Greta knew his name and waved hello to him every morning. When he sees us, his arms drop to his sides. "**Lo siento**," he says mournfully. For the only time in our relationship, we hug. We move through the lobby and into the elevator feeling eerily unencumbered.

We push the apartment door open and are greeted by silence. Nothing in here knows about Greta's death—not her red horsey with its empty smile, the toy bin beneath the living room chair, the straps on her purple high chair that she would fiddle with. We bring the news with us into each room, like smallpox.

Into this new, terminal stillness, a single buzzing fly emerges. We open all the windows, hoping the breeze will guide it out, then sit and listen as it bumps its head against the sill in the quiet. Neither of us can bring ourselves to suggest killing it. We are remembering the fly trapped in the apartment two weeks ago and how fascinated Greta was by its presence. She tracked its progress with wide eyes, her bare feet slapping on hardwood floors as it alit on every available surface. My hands itched to swat it, but her interest mounted with our irritation: "Where'd the fly go?" she asked us over and over.

It never failed; whatever made us grouchy drew her attention, until we were forced to grit our teeth and endure it. It was a toddler's natural response to fellow nuisances, and there seemed to be some mischief or wisdom behind it: she found the places in us that were small and pushed until we grew bigger. The returning fly felt like a practical joke and a reminder: **When you are at your most uncomfortable, your most irritable and small-minded; when you feel gripped by the worst of your impulses, remember—I am still here.**

We hear the fly buzz for a full week, as guests come and go, as our apartment fills and empties with families and meals.

✧

Extended family arrives that first evening— my aunt and cousins, my mother's side. They come in together, bravely dry-eyed, and hug me tight without saying much. I imagine they all met beforehand and agreed: no crying in front of Jayson and Stacy. We have a dinner party of sorts. I keep records playing constantly: lighthearted stuff, driving beats and bright voices. The table fills with empty wine bottles. My Brooklyn neighbors chatter merrily with my Niagara Falls cousins; parents of Greta's daycare friends joke with my mother. Jack is playing guitar again, and my father crouches at his feet like a small boy, the two of them harmonizing.

Watching my father, I feel a surge of tenderness that is almost protective. He is a pure soul, in both his unthinking generosity and his heedless enthusiasms. He always senses the emotional temperature of the room—even if he isn't quite sure what to do about it.

"Your father keeps coming up to me and whispering things," Stacy's friend Liz reports to me, sinking next to me on the couch and following my eyes to him. "He follows me from room to room, tugging at my arm and saying something completely unintelligible. Any idea what that might be?"

I shake my head wryly.

Stacy and I had always yearned for just this sort of effortless unity—everyone we had ever known, laughing and chatting, the threads around our spindle. Everyone Greta ever loved is here right now. It would have been the greatest party of her life.

I slip away and push open the door to Greta's room. I sit on her orange-striped couch, murmuring quietly to her. I give her a roll call of everyone she's missing. I promise to talk to her every day. I look around her room: her crib, stripped of her blankets and stuffed animals; her blue bookcase, covered in dollar-store stickers from an early-morning play session. I had just bought her the Frog and Toad books; she was too young for them still. I open my mouth again and then hesitate. Words sufficed when she was here to hear them, when every word was a pellet I deposited somewhere into that wondrous head, another penny in the bank. Here in the big empty room, they no longer serve me, or her.

Our family departs reluctantly to stay in a hotel, leaving John to watch over us. He keeps a miserable vigil on the couch while Stacy and I sob in bed. Sufjan Stevens's **Carrie & Lowell,** a record that had come out recently, spins quietly in the living room. It is music about death and about family: "We're all gonna die," Stevens whispers repeatedly on one song. My head and my heart are blank spaces.

Everything that happens to me in the next several days feels like rumor, supposition. Recalling it later is like trying to hack through bedrock—once lava cools and hardens, it just becomes the landscape.

I know that I allow my decisions to be made, my plate to be filled, my path to be cleared. At the periphery of my awareness, I sense Liz and Anna planning a memorial service for us. My grief has knocked me over decisively, and there is some comfort in the world's immediate and unanimous acknowledgment: I am like a big fallen tree being dotted with lichens and mushrooms.

Stacy, meanwhile, is trying to decide which photos of Greta will be best to print and hang at the venue. Somehow, we have never printed a picture of Greta: just another project we put off because we were sure we had the time. She scrolls through hundreds, thousands of photos, laptop balanced on her legs, trying to settle on the spread. **Are enough relatives pictured? Jayson's aunt and uncle will be at the service, can someone find the photo of them with Greta? We always liked her in this dress—let's find one of her wearing it.**

As she debates these minutiae with Liz sitting next to her on the couch, pulling nearby friends and cousins into the conversation, I catch myself glancing at her out of the corner of my eye with awe and concern. **Does anyone else hear her screaming silently through this?** I wonder.

✧

I am grieving around our apartment like a man from an Old World painting—wailing, ripped garments, balled fists—but Stacy's trauma is not as readily evident. Like any born empath, she considers her own feelings to be the third or fourth most interesting thing in the room. Her emotions, as a result, are private, wordless things, more sound and sensation than conscious thought. They escape her strict surveillance only in jagged bursts, under cover of convenient distractions:

her outsized consternation at a plate of runny eggs, a malfunctioning dryer, a late bus.

Sitting on the couch, sifting through Greta's photos, her expression is so sharp and clear, her voice so calm, that a stranger would never know she's a grieving mother, a figure so awful it's almost primeval. But it's a trick of the light, and only I see the gruesome scarring and open wounds covering her body.

The issue consuming her at the moment is how to reconcile the two separate funeral guest lists: one of them for the service and one for the luncheon. Who is a service-only person? Who should be invited to the luncheon? The names swarm on a two-tabbed document in front of Stacy like microbes on a petri dish. Overwhelmed, she throws up her hands and cries helplessly, "This is the worst thing ever!"

Liz, eyeing her, deadpans, "I don't think so."

They both start giggling, high and manic.

✧

We are huddled in the apartment one morning, somewhere in the middle of our makeshift **shiva**, when I stand up abruptly.

I am drowning in the air of the apartment, surrounded by the couch and chairs Greta climbed on. "I think I'm going for a walk," I announce. "I'd like us to have some more wine for dinner."

My family watches me, wary. "Are you sure you want to go by yourself?" Stacy asks.

"I am, I think. Just a few bottles. I'll take my phone."

I set off down the stairs, taking them two at a time in my relief.

The minute I get outside, though, I sense the depth of my misjudgment. Everywhere I look, I am blinded by her. There is Greta, running up ahead of me to the corner, rounding at the fence to go to her friend Jacob's house. There she is stomping gleefully through the patches of "dirty dirt" surrounding the trees on our street. Each sidewalk crack is one I recall rolling stroller wheels over while she slept, pressing down on the handle to keep it from bouncing her.

I turn left at the first chance and realize this is the route to the park. Just a week ago we came this way while she hollered "The Wheels on the Bus."

I push tears away angrily with the heel of my palm, veering back onto the main street before realizing the playground is just up ahead. I feel like an escaped zoo animal stranded on a four-lane superhighway. The sun bears down on me like a klieg light.

A hand touches my shoulder: "Jayson." It is our neighbor Oren, the father of Greta's friend Ayelet, who lives two floors above us in our building. The two were odd playmates— Ayelet is coltish and giggly, where Greta was sly and prone to sitting—but they shrieked with pleasure when they saw each other.

My expression is an open wound I don't have the presence of mind or time to rearrange into something more presentable, but he receives the look with an alert calm. "What are you doing, Jayson?" he asks, light and curious.

"We needed more wine," I mutter, gesturing up the block. "I was just going to go pick it up."

"More . . . wine," Oren says slowly, processing the nature of my errand. "OK, well. How about I pick up a bottle for you? I can bring it back. What would you like?"

I stare at him, dumb.

"It really isn't a problem at all. Why don't you go back home? I can drop it off at your door."

I hesitate, then dig in my track pants for the twenties I'd brought before he shushes me, puts a hand on my shoulder, and steers me back. "Don't worry about it," he says.

I call my therapist. "She's **everywhere I look!**" I shriek, pressing my hand to my temple as if to keep a vein from bursting. I gaze up; the wind ripples through the trees. I can see every single leaf articulated on every single branch, fluttering. My therapist is talking; I focus on the voice in my phone.

"You're being flooded, Jayson," she says calmly. "You should go home now, and you should stay there for a while. There will be a time to test your boundaries, but now is not that time. Go home."

I hang up the phone, drained and numb.

Five steps from my front door, I spot them: two women sitting in a parked car across the street, eating something out of a bag. They see me and stop eating. I slow my walk, feeling a pit form. In addition to the forbidding note plastered on our door, an email has gone around our building, urging neighbors to keep silent in the face of the press. Gazing at the women in the car, I am suddenly impatient with all this protection. I stop and lock eyes with the woman in the passenger seat.

Her eyes widen in surprise and then turn quizzical: **Should we?** I wave her over with agitation: **Yes, yes, come on, let's do this.** They are suddenly all business, the bag abandoned and recorders grabbed and doors opened in simultaneous awkward haste. I watch them gather themselves, set their facial expressions, and cross the street.

The shorter woman has soft, pained eyes, and she holds her recorder far from her body, as if it were unclean. "Whatever you want to say to us," she says. "Whether it's 'leave me alone' or something more. We can also leave if you want us to." I wonder if she has been waiting for someone to give her permission to go away all day.

"Thank you," I say. I fight back a sense of foolishness. "I have a statement on my phone, I'd just like to read it." I pull my phone out and notice that my hand is trembling. I look down studiously and read: "This is a devastating loss. We are deeply grateful to the PICU team at Weill Cornell for their efforts on her behalf." I pause, take a deep, jagged breath. "My family requests the basic dignity of privacy and space as we grieve. Thank you." I look up at them and try to control my face, which I can feel twitching.

"How is your wife?" one of them asks. "How is the grandmother?"

I back away, suddenly aware of the sun in my eyes, the passersby on the street. "I . . . I'm just going to go back upstairs to my family," I say. They are still talking. I say thank you again over my shoulder and push open the door.

Two hours later, the story appears: I am described as "shattered," and in the headline I am "pleading" for privacy. I shut my laptop with grim satisfaction; I have handled something.

✧

Greta's service takes place on Saturday, six days after the accident, at a Quaker school.

The meetinghouse is spacious and light, with cream walls. Downstairs, hundreds of photos of Greta are strung up on clotheslines, the result of Stacy's labors. Croissants and danishes, cut-up fruit and coffee. Upstairs, there is a single framed picture in the middle of the room, next to a bouquet of flowers. My mother took it, and we all agree it captures Greta perfectly: she smiles up at the camera, mischievous, from beneath the canopy of a tree. It looks like the sort of place we hope she's in now.

I'm wearing the tan suit I got married in, a steel-blue shirt underneath. I struggled getting dressed, trying on two shirts and taking them off. I wasn't entirely sure what I was going for—how do you dress for your daughter's funeral?—but I knew I didn't want to look like I needed help.

Now, watching mourners and extended family stream into the schoolhouse, I feel oddly at ease. I have lived in a world with my dead daughter in it for 144 hours, and it feels like my duty to shepherd these shocked faces into the new reality.

It is gruesome and unimaginable, what we

are doing, and yet there is something beautiful in it, too. Standing in the entryway, like a rock in a river, I greet friends I haven't seen in years, coworkers, and acquaintances, all surging forward to embrace me. I have the queer sensation that I am attending my own funeral. **Now I know exactly what people will say,** I think. **They are saying it to me now.**

We have no religion, Stacy and I. When it comes to spiritual matters we are cultural freeloaders, picking off other people's plates. For our wedding vows, we adapted language from the ketubah, the Jewish marriage contract. Neither of us is Jewish: my father left behind his Jewish upbringing with his other youthful unhappinesses, and Susan was a fierce atheist in a largely Christian Virginia suburb during Stacy's childhood. Their ranch house was catty-corner from an evangelical church, and Susan would arm Stacy with directives before playdates with the church-attending children: "OK, this time, ask them about Adam and Eve's two sons. Where did their **wives** come from?" In high school, Stacy sported the Darwin fish in her rear windshield, a small defiance cheered by Susan.

But we found the ketubah to be a heart-eningly practical document, full of good language about how to live well together. We even stepped on a glass to conclude the ceremony, but mindful that the crunch might resound painfully in my father's ears, I sat down and wrote out some language carefully couching it as something nonreligious, a piece of symbolism we were claiming for our own. In the closing lines of our vows, we made a promise to each other that washes back up now with eerie prescience: **"I know we will face difficulties we cannot foresee, but I have faith we will confront them together and never lose sight of each other."**

Now that Greta is dead, we find ourselves once again reaching for the traditions of others. A college girlfriend of mine was raised Quaker, and I was always intrigued by her descriptions of the ceremony, in which participants rise to speak only when the spirit moves them.

"Man, isn't that weird?" I asked. "What do you do during the silences? Do you just stare at your hands the whole time?"

"You just sit," my girlfriend said. "It's not weird."

We discovered the ceremony's power at a friend's wedding, two years before Greta was born. Stacy and I took seats near the front of the room, both anxious. Neither of us was accustomed to the idea of letting silences go unfilled, and we were taking bets on who would be first between us to stand up and blurt out something horrifying.

Thankfully, others knew their way around this dance, and as they rose, spoke, and slowly seated themselves, the room's silence began to feel hypnotic. Friends, family, and teachers told stories, shared memories, drew laughs—a natural harmony emerged, like overtones shimmering from a plucked string. Stacy and I caught each other's eye in wonder. I even rose to say something, moved only by inspiration. I don't recall a word, but I can still feel the warmth that flooded me upon sitting down.

At Greta's memorial, Stacy and I sit in the front row at the center of the room. From here, the seating radiates outward in all directions, enclosing us.

There is a rustle, the sound of a roomful of people becoming aware of a holdup: we can't begin without Susan. The only way into the room is up a flight of stairs—no elevator or ramp—and with her injured legs, she can't climb them. As we sit in the meeting room, Susan is forced to climb into an archaic motorized chair running up the bannister, one that groans when it switches on. We wait inside, the hum from the stairs faintly audible, and I am glad for Susan's sake and mine that we aren't witnessing her awkward ascent. After a long minute, she appears at the back entrance, limping and trying to slide into her seat next to Stacy while escaping notice. I feel her suppress a groan as she settles.

Danny takes his spot in front of the assemblage. He was Stacy's professor at New England Conservatory, which means he knew her before I did. When we were dating, he was the first father figure of hers I met, and I felt his keenly appraising eye when we shook hands. He was a natural choice for our master of ceremonies, the kind of person who speaks in expansive, generous paragraphs without seeming to try.

"What I see when I look around today is a system," he says. "And I see that system activating today. It is our duty to surround these two generous and wonderful people with all the love we have."

My mother stands to speak first, and I realize with some astonishment how still and quiet she is. Normally, she never stops moving, striding where others merely walk and leaving the air quivering behind her.

She looks heartbreakingly cut down to size; her cheeks are hollowed out and she stands rigid with the effort of keeping her composure. Her granddaughter's death seems to have altered the weight of gravity on her frame. "Greta radiated charisma," she says, reading from a small handwritten sheet of ruled paper. "She had a mysterious glint in her eye—you always wanted to know what she was thinking. She lit up a room just by walking into it, and everyone wanted to be near her, to simply be where she was. I want to remember all the joy she brought whenever I think of her, because she would not want us to be sad."

My brother goes next, and I sense he is

also holding himself together out of pure will. They are steely people, John and my mother—task executioners, people who get things done. In the past four days, John has flown back to Colorado to move into a new house, a move he put on hold when I called him from the emergency room. He returned with his wife and two kids on the day of the funeral. He wrote his speech on the plane. Giving John a task is like hitching a sled to a mountain dog: he throws every muscle and sinew into it gratefully, as if the performance relieves some primal pressure of his existence.

Today, John speaks clearly and calmly, his feet spaced apart and his arms spread wide, as if to enfold us all.

"The things I saw in the hospital this week were some of the hardest, most painful and awful of my life," he says. "But I will tell you I also saw some of the most amazing, the most loving, the most benevolent acts. They were things I could not have imagined, and they have left me humbled and awestruck. Stacy lying in the bed with Greta, cradling her broken child to her for as long as she still could. Immense acts of kindness from the hospital staff, who I expected to be colder, harder from their difficult environment. And finally the brave decision by Stacy and Jayson to pass on what they could from their daughter to save other young lives."

He looks up from his notes, seeming to fix each of us with his gaze. "I stand with you today broken, filled with grief and sorrow. But I am so grateful for all of you, for your support to endure this. I don't know how to get through this, but I know that we will, and that we will do it together."

It is my turn to speak; I read a letter to Greta. I wrote it last night. "In the ultimate analysis, Stacy and I were the people who loved each other enough to bring Greta Greene into this world," I say. "You were all the people who loved her, shaped her, and invited her into the world. How could we all not be overwhelmingly proud of that fact?"

After I finish, the room opens to anyone who may feel moved to contribute. There is a heavy silence, punctured by my friend Ben sharing a light story about Greta glaring at him and declaring, "You are not my daddy." The floodgates open after that. Cousins speak;

friends speak. Our friend Jenna, an English teacher, reads a remark from Isabel Allende on surviving the death of her adult daughter, Paula: "We learn to live with the sadness like a great, lovely companion, because it's a soft sadness that softens the heart and makes you open to everything."

Three of Greta's daycare providers stand together and tell stories about her. "One day, Greta was playing next to a friend, and the friend passed gas," says a woman named Toyana. "Greta looked at me and said, 'Toyana, she burped in her butt!'" Stacy squeezes my hand and we both laugh. Greta was a connoisseur of bathroom humor.

As the ceremony goes on, I can sense the accumulated weight of our grief in the room and our power in sharing it. We are passing through some sort of magnificent, terrible threshold together. We are headed toward something; I don't know where it is leading, but the incipient knowledge is like a ringing in my ears.

Stacy sits silent at my side. She is wearing a gorgeous peach-colored dress, sleeveless with large printed white flowers. She bought it the day we dropped Greta off with Susan, Greta's last day.

I sneak glances at her and Susan occasionally, daughter and mother. I wonder if their proximity just now is hard for Stacy: Susan is currently more haunted spirit than human being, trapped inside an exquisite private hell that even I flinch from imagining. There is so much that needs to be said between them, so much that never can be.

I feel certain that Stacy will not—cannot—speak in these circumstances. It is her first time out of the apartment since we came home from the hospital. My mother, brother, and I planned speeches, but Stacy had intentionally not prepared one. Public speaking isn't in her nature. Instead she burrows into projects. The photos, and the natural way they diffused attention, are more her style. She has encouraged people to take home photos they love—to help spread Greta's spirit, she tells me.

And yet, just as Danny motions for us to wrap things up, Stacy stands, shakily. Her face is pale, but her eyes are blazing. Everything and everyone she has ever been in her life—

daughter, sister, colleague, wife, mother—is visible to me. She is overwhelmingly beautiful in this moment.

"As many of you know, I'm not much of a public speaker," she begins. The room laughs gently. She opens with a story about taking Greta to see Susan the day before the accident. She took their last day for granted, she says, and spent most of it grumpy and impatient. Greta was upset with her when she was upset. She regrets it now.

Then she starts to tell stories of Susan and Greta, of their relationship and their time together. As she speaks, it dawns on me what she is doing, maybe why she stood to speak: Stacy is publicly absolving her mother. I look at her in wonder, and it occurs to me again how little knowledge I have of the inner workings of her heart.

I sense now that she is summoning the version of the truth she needs—maybe the truth we all need, in order to survive—from deep within herself. The task feels Herculean, a boulder lifted overhead.

"Grandma Suz was one of her favorite people in the world," Stacy says, turning to look at her mother directly. "We had been promising her she would come visit you all last week, and she was so excited. She wanted nothing more than to spend time with her Grandma Suz. She had **the best day**," she finishes, her eyes filling and her voice breaking. She sits down, spent from effort.

✧

When the service ends, fleets of cars take people to a pizzeria down the block from our apartment. Guests mill about, drinking beers, taking their glasses out to the sidewalk. My boss bullshits with my father about the Beach Boys, my coworkers grab my parents and hug them before introducing themselves. Everyone seems elated by the improbable grace of what has just happened. I am sitting in the back when my sister-in-law, Melissa, approaches me, her eyes shining with tears. "We weren't so sure you would ever be able to navigate the big city," she kids me tearily. "But look at this," she says, and she waves a wondering hand around her, at all the friends and life around us.

After the party dies down, everyone resumes the vigil at our apartment. Some gather in the living room, some in the kitchen, picking over food. The afternoon light is saddening, draining the last of our euphoria with it.

Ten, maybe fifteen of us sit on the floor in Greta's room, me leaning against the blue bookcase. Light streams in through both windows. Jack, sitting cross-legged in the middle of the room, is once again playing guitar—it is something useful, something he can offer.

He strums softly, singing under his breath. Wilco songs, Gram Parsons songs—the soundtrack to his and Stacy's childhood. Then, with a knowing, pained look in my direction, he starts playing the chords to "Between the Bars" by Elliott Smith. It is a dark song, but only if you pay attention to the words; its melody is soft and loping, and I sang a modified version of it to Greta every night, her head on my shoulder, as she gradually grew heavier and allowed herself to surrender to unconsciousness. Jack is playing it for me.

I sang it to Greta because "I'll kiss you again / Between the bars" suggests a kiss through a crib as easily as two lovers separated by a jail cell, or drunkards pausing in their pub crawl. I thought of its final image— "People you've been before / That you don't want around anymore / That push and shove and won't bend to your will / I'll keep them still"—as a promise I made to her that only I understood the meaning of. **Whoever you want to become: I am only here to clear your path.**

I strategically changed other lyrics as well— "stay up all night" became "sleep through the night"—but there is an unchanged lyric that haunts me now: "The potential you'll be / That you'll never see." Sitting in my dead daughter's bedroom, on the floor in front of her empty crib, they strike me as dreadful words to sing to a child, a curse laid on a life full of promise.

I close my eyes and begin to sing it: I can smell her. The tufty fuzz of her hair as it bristled against my ear; the reassuring weight of her bottom pressing down on my forearm, the softness of her diaper tangible through her pajama pants. My other hand on the sweatshirt she wore. When she was ready, truly ready, to be laid down in the crib, I could feel a subtle shift—her joints would loosen, her muscles softening. She became pliable, and as I would lean her over her mattress, her head would drop back and her legs would curl, like an itinerant aircraft docking at a space station.

The song ends, and I trail off. After a moment, Lesley softly says, because someone has to say something, "That was nice, Jayson." I know it is the last time I will ever sing that song.

✦

As the days inch forward, the tide of visitors recedes, a few at a time. John flies back to Colorado; my friend Anna leaves for Ohio. Our little village is loosening its tight grip on us, and sooner rather than later, Stacy and I will be alone.

My parents leave last. Hugging me, my mother finally allows herself to shatter completely, sobbing in my arms. I hold her close and feel her thinness, her smallness, so easy to overlook in the blare of her personality, and think, **Here you are.** We had once been so close, my mother and I. At some point during my adolescence, we had wrenched ourselves apart, and we had never really found our way back.

My mother pulls herself upright, her vulnerability already a distant memory. Having learned to be tough early, she's never unlearned it: indomitable once more.

My father trails her mournfully, unable to look me in the eye for long. When I hug him good-bye, he grips me tightly, as if he is trying to hold me together. But I sense, when he lets go of me, he will be adrift. The two of them linger in the doorway, hesitant, but there is nowhere else to go, nothing else to be done. The door closes with a **click.** Stacy and I are left to whatever will become of our lives.

That night, we surprise ourselves, grabbing for each other on the couch and falling into an urgent, hungry kind of sex. We both weep; then we both crawl into bed, clasping hands and whispering, "Good night, Greta." We slip beneath the glassy surface of a sleep that still contains no dreams. We sleep late. We sleep late every morning now.

Friends continue to bring us food over the next several days, and we eat, continuously, ravenously, everything that spills over our refrigerator shelves. We fill our senses with cold grapes, hot stew, toasted bagels overflowing with cream cheese—anything to drown out the new roaring silence in our apartment.

Stacy punctures that silence our second night alone, playing a video of Greta on her phone. I have resisted the videos, aware of the damage they could do, but hearing her little voice emerge from the tiny phone speaker, some part of me wants to stick a finger in the open wound, root around until I find a live nerve. I walk over to Stacy: "Play it again."

In the video, Greta is wearing sweatpants but no shirt. It is at some jittery, monkeyish point right before bedtime, and she is singing "The Farmer in the Dell," substituting her best friend's name, Eva, for "farmer." It sounds like "Eva and the day," and it's a version of the song she learned in her daycare in the mornings, during "circle time," a way to welcome everyone to the morning.

I had completely forgotten about that song and the way she sang it, and that realization, coupled with the shock and devastation of seeing her moving and singing again, sends me sobbing to the floor. I wonder: **What else have I already forgotten? What other songs did she sing?**

I open my laptop and begin writing memories down frantically. I recall watching her learn how to crawl, one limb at a time, reaching one hand into the air as she tentatively moved her back legs. It took her ages—for an infant's mental timeline, she must have felt like she had been learning to crawl for a thousand years. But her focus was quiet and unrelenting; she never whined or fussed. She simply learned. Meditative, curious, absorbed: How much closer am I **now**?

She loved to comfort. If I muttered about something, she'd walk up to me: "Daddy, what's wrong wif you?" I would say, "Nothing, baby girl, Daddy's just frustrated," and she'd pat me on the shoulder and assure me, "It's OK, Daddy."

She was anything beautiful I ever found in myself or the world around me, in addition to all the things she was all on her own: stubborn, protective, mischievous, strong-willed, curious. She had a certain hardened-forehead way of determining exactly what was right for her; "You are a force of nature, baby girl," Stacy told her, laughing, at ten months.

She was uncomfortable with crowds, as was I. The only exception was family: with family, there could never be too much. One of the last things she'd do before finally surrendering to sleep was to recite a roll call into the dark of all the people she loved.

How could we have failed this little person so completely?

✧

Greta's body is released from the medical examiner and delivered to a funeral home in Midtown Manhattan. Joe, a shaky and discomfited man with gold cuff links, sits across from us at his walnut desk on top of bloodred carpeting. This is where she is.

Someone from the funeral home—someone who wasn't Joe—told us on the phone that if we wished to say good-bye to her body before it was incinerated, we could do so. Joe is deeply disturbed by this and makes no attempt to hide it. Her body was compromised, he tells us. Organs had been removed. She was small to begin with. Her body stayed at the medical examiner's office for a week for the autopsy. There wasn't, he makes clear, much of her left to say good-bye to.

My stomach balls in disgust as Joe's eyes offer a wet approximation of sympathy. "Look, I don't know who told you you could see her," he says. "But you have to trust me: you don't want to see her. It's best you remember her the way she was."

⟡

Two weeks after coming home, we go back to work. The timing is absurd, barbaric. But when you are in shock, just about any activity seems perfectly reasonable. Our respective bosses assure us we can take all the time we need, but we feel an instinctive urge to plow headlong into groups of people, to be handed projects.

Stacy's job has an extra complication: she left the music industry four years ago, went back to school, and is now a dietitian and lactation consultant working for WIC, a program providing care for the children of low-income parents. Each morning, she faces an endless tide of newborns and toddlers Greta's age. She never tells any of these new mothers about Greta. I do not understand her ability to handle infants, to kneel and talk to other people's toddlers, day after day, after watching our daughter be wheeled away—it is beyond my comprehension.

It is also somewhat beyond hers, she admits. The most sense she can make of it: "I mean, a baby never makes you feel **bad**. It's impossible to feel bad around a baby." I am stunned, but I also can't argue with her.

There is something comforting in the blankness of the bureaucracy, she says. She checks boxes, reminds everyone to eat fruits and vegetables. She counsels new parents through the overwhelming predicaments of newborn life, losing herself in the all-consuming nature of their problems: **How often should my baby breastfeed? How many wet diapers should she have on day six? How will we get through the next twenty-four hours?** In this way she is able to sublimate her own grief, or even forget it for a few hours. Only when she's in the car does she cry and cry.

Occasionally she will look up from her desk and find herself staring at a boy or girl with Greta's birthday. It hurts, but she also welcomes the chance to speak to someone from Greta's little tribe.

I return to my editor position at Pitchfork, a website where I've freelanced for years. Like Stacy, I am new, only three months in. On my first day, I sit on the subway feeling bruised all over, like I might burst into tears if someone poked me. People at my office wince when they see me; they treat me with extraordinary kindness and care, but I feel them suppressing shudders behind my back.

I am ice-skating along the surface of my shock, and nothing I do seems unusual or beyond the pale. No one expects anything from me. I come to work, or I don't. I slip in and out of the office, disappearing halfway through the day if I need to with nothing but a text to a coworker. It is a tremendous and scary freedom.

I learn something hidden and unpleasant about my chosen profession in these weeks.

Yes, listening to music can be life affirming, a conduit to your deepest emotions. It can also be simply noise, a horse blanket blotting out sensation.

There is one album, by two young women in L.A. who call themselves Girlpool, that pierces the ice. It is campfire music, two guitar chords hinted at by fingers and lyrics about the dawning realizations of youth, the ones that feel like sunrise on your entire brain. I keep one song close, called "I Like That You Can See It." I try to hold this thought in front of me.

My second full week back, I go out at night. A singer-songwriter named Mitski is playing a tiny stage. She overwhelms it completely, feet planted far apart, hair tossed back, eyes burning into individual members of her audience. I stand near the back behind my coworker Jenn, who booked the show. Mitski closes with what is then her signature anthem, a feedback-soaked rock song that climaxes with the line "I'm not gonna be what my daddy wants me to be / I wanna be what my body wants me to be." I am exhilarated even as I realize in that moment that Greta will never have a profound moment of self-expression like Mitski's or live a life like Jenn's, full of art and possibility.

✧

Apart from brief moments like these, time passes mostly soundlessly. There are days when I am confused, panicked, like I've woken up in a dark room with unfamiliar contours: **What is it? What is it that feels so awful?** Then I calm down and I remember: **Oh yes, I am in hell.** The thought places me in time and space, like a dot dropped on a map. Once I am armed with this knowledge, my eyes clear, my walk straightens, my breathing slows.

Having exited the blaze of grief standing upright, we now find ourselves flattened by its drudgery. We go to work every day and then discuss the problems we tackled at a different restaurant every night, over food we barely taste. We drink wine, but not too much. We watch a few hours of one show or another, then go to bed, then sleep past 8:00 a.m. every day. We do not scream at anyone. Neither of us gets sick.

As long as your situation is unique, exceptional, there always remains the chance that things will revert back to "normal" if only you have the strength to endure it. "Haven't we done this long enough?" Stacy sometimes says plaintively. "Can't we have her back now?"

Everyone tells us they are in awe of us. "I am in awe of your strength," friends tell us. "You two are an inspiration." I grow to hate the sound of these words, a steady drip from a faucet I want to yank shut with a wrench. "I feel like a coma patient being congratulated for not dying," I tell Stacy.

Even worse than this ever-present concern and attention is the looming threat that it might disappear. **He seems to want everything to go back to normal,** my friends and coworkers reasonably conclude from my behavior. I keep coming in to work. I keep social engagements. I text jokes to friends. I follow the news; I comment. I buy new clothes, nice ones, and new glasses. I sense myself sending a signal out into the world, determined and stubborn: **I am not some broken man.** But I am not sure I want anyone to believe me.

On the one hand, coping with loss under a spotlight is intolerable. On the other hand, there is succor to be drawn from all that awe and care. I am playing hurt, after all. Some part of me wants that to go on forever: for the game to go on but remain solemnly rigged in my favor. The standing ovation, the hero's welcome, the defensive line that dissolves when I approach it—I want it all to continue indefinitely. The idea that things will go back to normal—that I will be expected not only to keep on living but to gamely leap hurdles—tax season, crowded commutes, deadlines—makes me think about how the real pain isn't in the leg being mangled. It's in the way the bone sets.

✧

By the second month, the overwhelming urge to die that I felt in the hospital subsides to an ache. My longing for death is now something I simply carry around with me, like hay fever.

Raymond Carver once wrote, of a character in one of his stories, that he "understood that he was willing to be dead," and that's it. The flash, the drama, the moment of passage or transition, the cries of grief of my loved ones and family, the funeral—none of that intrigues me. I am simply interested in the state of **being** dead, the cessation of all further sensations and thoughts and experiences. That seems entirely reasonable to me, even pleasant, like leaning into a roaring fire and letting it wash away your senses.

I deal with this suicidal despair the way you might endure a terrible pain in your side post-op: it is a necessary condition for the state I'm in. Nothing seems strange or even upsetting about this feeling; in fact, it is one of the most normal ones I have, and there is comfort in just how logical it is. It's just one more thing that flares up when I am tired or stressed, a knot that tenses and then relaxes as I count breaths.

Sometimes, at lunch hour, I will walk down to the pier near our workspace. There is a thinly populated, patchy field only a three-minute walk from the office. There is always a risk of running into other coworkers. But I treat this park like a sanctuary, and often I go and lie down on my back, just beneath a little sapling tree, and gaze up at the sky to weep. Other times I walk up to the sharp rocks just before the water, letting the breeze pound my face. It is easier there to come unwound, to holler into the water.

"Oh, sweetie, I'm so angry," I sob. "I look for you everywhere I go. You would have been talking so much. You were two years old when that chunk of brick hit you."

I look up and scream, "In the head! It hit you in the fucking head! It was still growing little hairs on it." I blubber; I mewl. I yell at no one: "Why did you do this to us? Why did you do it to her? She was two years old. Why did you do it?"

There is no one to talk to, no single person to blame. I listen to the waves pound. A breeze stirs my arm hairs. I cover my face with my hands and press hard. I hear the waves; I smell the pungent harbor. I breathe jaggedly until I breathe slowly. Then I turn around and walk back to the office and sit down at my computer and answer thirty emails.

I am a bereaved father. My only child died when she was two. She was struck in the head by a brick that fell off a building. Sometimes I hear these sentences dancing across my mind to the sound of my typing. I wonder how many times I will have to say them for the rest of my life.

"Yeah, sounds good," I tell a writer who is filing late.

"No update on that one," I write to a publicist who is just circling back on this Nashville band: they'd obviously be thrilled if a review was happening; they are wondering if I've gotten around to giving it a spin yet.

"I really think we should cover this one," I write, hitting "forward" on an album stream to a few other editors sitting feet away from me.

Greta was the victim of an accident. An accident happened. I have to learn to state this grievously unacceptable information over and over again. In every interaction, I am the messenger for a rip in the universe, a talisman that carries the message "All will not be well" with me into every new room. I am the reminder of the most unwelcome message in human history: Children—yours, mine—they don't necessarily live.

✧

I am working in a café across the street from a middle school. Bright, chatty, headstrong children regularly fill it in the hours just before school starts.

"Wait—who forced whose hand into a pile of poo?" I hear a voice say, a female voice. I look up. A young woman has pushed open the door to the coffee shop, trailing two excitable boys with her, maybe eight and ten.

"Sasha did—to Porter," squeals one of the boys, pointing at the other. They collapse in fits of giggles.

The woman smiles patiently, rolling her eyes for comic effect. "That's disgusting, Sasha," she said. "I bet your mother loved that."

She is a regular babysitter, maybe, or a younger aunt. She is in charge of them, at any rate, and from their body language they have spent countless hours in one another's company.

She buys them croissants, and they sit down at a table near me, the two boys picking at the pastries distractedly and jabbing each other. I have my headphones in, but there is no music in them, so their voices come through slightly muffled and aquatic. I can warm my hands on their little scene without being noticed. The other boy has apparently written a short story for school in which Prince has a cameo.

"That's amazing," the young woman says, shaking her head in admiration. "Having Prince as a character in your short story is hilarious."

"Hopefully we'll always be your favorite kids," the boy says, and it's clear they are hopelessly in love with her, as anyone would be. I want to be her, basking in their slipstream of unconditional affection.

Behind them, I recognize a mother at a table whose child goes to Greta's daycare—Lucy's mom, maybe. She is meeting with a woman I don't recognize. The woman is complaining idly to her about their child's kindergarten teacher. "Don't get me wrong, Ms. Deborah is amazing, Maddie loves her. I just wish there weren't so many parties. There were **three** birthday parties this week, which means Maddie had cupcakes for lunch three days in a row. She basically has a sugar crash the minute I see her. But I don't want to be the mom who banned cupcakes, you know?"

I stare at them and am startled to discover I loathe them. The language they speak used to be my language, my everyday words. Now I have new everyday words—"skull surgery," "brain trauma"—and they taste like volcanic ash in my mouth. I hate each and every one of them: their unexamined happiness, the unspeakable luxury they have to still worry about cupcakes. I wish monstrous things on them and their families.

I am horrified by all this newly evident bile in my soul. It pours out of me now, a new waste product of my existence. I regard it with dismay like water pouring through a hole in a once-secure boat: no matter how hastily I bail, there is always more when I reach down.

I leave the café and hurry to the train. Only when the doors open do I realize, with dread, that I am stepping onto a train populated by small children. I steel myself and step in, feeling their disinterested gazes burn me.

This is Brooklyn, spilling over with toddlers and happy families, and it has become intolerable. Children pass me everywhere, trailing echoes, babbling at me with their potential futures. Occasionally, I find myself making funny faces at one of them to see them giggle. I am at war with myself in these moments, taking furtive pleasure in their delighted responses while bracing myself for the inevitable question: "Do you have kids?"

Stacy and I talk a lot about this question. In responding, she gauges the depth of the conversation she's having, the likelihood she will ever speak to this person again. She will not tell the checkout clerk at the grocery store or the woman selling her hand cream that, yes, she did in fact have a child once, but she died in a freak accident a month or so ago. Oh, and should she insert her card here or swipe it?

Stacy simply says no and leaves everyone unscathed and unimplicated. Me, I opt for the hard way every single time, with all the stricken faces and the "I'm so sorrys" this implies. I take guilty, grim satisfaction in being able to blamelessly detonate this grenade in the lives of strangers. It is a cruel and ungenerous leg sweep in response to a question born only of fellowship and human curiosity. "Yeah, I had a fucking kid. She died. Have a pleasant afternoon."

I go to a yoga class every day, feeling hot tears spread down my face during the resting meditation at the end of every class. But no matter how diligently I tunnel, I'm aware of just keeping my hands and head busy. Grief, on this level, is simply something that happens to you, a series of events that passes through you, like a birth. It is bigger and deeper than any single coherent thought. **When you're this hurt, this is what twiddling your thumbs looks like,** I think.

✧

Ever since the accident, I have avoided going to the park. The park was our place, Greta's and mine—every tree, every leaf, every passing doggy belonged to the two of us. Even within my cocoon of shock, I am sure going there would pierce my defenses, flooding me the way my first trip outside did after she died.

And then, one day, just as the summer light is beginning to change, I wake up with a familiar itch. **I need to go running in the park.** I poke at the impulse, trying to determine if it's madness. But I feel different, stronger somehow. I change into shorts, tighten my sneakers, and queue up some propulsive, abrasive music on my phone.

I step outside and feel only the warmth of the sun. I round the corner on the block that leads to the parade grounds, just outside the park's southwest entrance. The street is wide, quiet, shaded. There is no one outside, no one to nod at, make eye contact with, step around.

I enter the parade grounds and run past fields full of children, my eyes fixed straight ahead. To my left, a middle school football team is doing speed and endurance drills, dancing frantically on their toes and dropping down for push-ups. Two boys swing a bat lazily to my right, smacking a baseball into the same bulged-out spot on the chain-link. It hits the fence with a loud **bong** as I run past, but I do not flinch. I reach the edge of the park, tennis courts to my right.

There at the park's mouth, my heart stirs, and I feel a peculiar elation. **I recognize her.** Greta is somewhere nearby. I feel her energy, playfully expectant. **Come find me, Daddy,** she says. Tears spring and run freely down my face. **I hear you, baby girl,** I whisper. **Daddy's coming to get you.**

Elated, I enter the park and immediately spot her; she is waiting for me, hiding behind the big tree in the clearing between the Vanderbilt playground and the duck pond. She appears from behind the tree with a flourish, giggling, just like in our old game: she would run out into the hallway from the bedroom where we had been playing, either naked or in her diaper, and cast me an impish look, asking, "Where's Greta?" I would feign great perplexity, turning over small toys on the floor to see if she was under them, peeking behind the couch, clutching my head in mock terror. "Oh no, what have we done?" I would moan. "We've lost her!" She would laugh, run back in, and announce, "Greta came right back!"

Standing in the park, staring at her, I make a strange and primal sound, deep and rich like a belly laugh, hard and sharp like a sob. **You are here. You picked the park. Good choice, baby girl.** Oblivious to the people around me, I run to her. She wiggles in anticipatory joy. Stooping down, I scoop her up under her soft armpits, her shoulder blades meeting at the pads of my fingers, and I lift her up into the sky. She is invisible to passersby—to them, there is nothing in the spot next to the tree where she stands laughing and clapping but a patch of grass, and there is nothing in my arms but air. But she is not here for them; she is here for me.

She gazes down at me, her smile that turned crooked at the bottom like mine crumpling her wide-open face. I bend my arms and lower her face down to mine and kiss her, slowly. Then I set her back down in the grass.

You stay here, OK? I say. **Daddy's going for a run, OK, sweetie pie?**

Oh yeah, OK! she says back.

I turn around and begin running hard along the perimeter of the pond, where we had dipped her hand in the water, splashing and saying, "Here we go, ducks! Here we go!" As I pump my limbs, my hamstrings groan and then open; my body awakens. The playground recedes behind me, where I had pushed her on the swing while she sang, "Poopy, poopy, poopy poopy," to the tune of "Twinkle, Twinkle, Little Star" at the top of her lungs. "If my kid's saying 'poopy' tonight," the mother next to me deadpanned, "I'll know where he picked it up."

As my chest swells like a bellows, I feel her presence filling up my heart, and with it comes a strange exhilaration that I have felt often in the weeks after her death. Grief at its peak has a terrible beauty to it, a blinding fission of every emotion. The world is charged with significance, with meaning, and the world around you, normally so solid and implacable, suddenly looks thin, translucent. I feel like I've discovered an opening. I don't know quite what's behind it yet. But it is there. I open up into a sprint, liberated.

I am treading ether, a new and unfamiliar kind of contact high. I have been raised secular by my parents, and I've never set foot in a church for more than an hour. But I will do anything for Greta, I am learning. And that includes becoming a mystic, so that I might still enjoy her company.

When I reach the edge of the park again, I stop and feel a torrent of words flood me. I grope for my phone, blindly choosing the most recent document, a mess of to-dos and grocery lists. Underneath a reminder to pick up pita and above a confirmation number for a UPS delivery, I write, "There will be more light upon this earth for me."

Three

KRIPALU

I STAND IN FRONT OF PETER, our eyes locked, our hands clasped in prayer. "I see your grief; I acknowledge your pain," he murmurs to me, his green eyes near frozen.

"I see your grief; I acknowledge your pain," I repeat back to him, struggling not to avert my eyes.

Peter is taller than me, with hair buzzed to his scalp and a blue-collar diffidence I can smell. We met eleven seconds ago, thrown together by our grief-group leader, and before even shaking hands, we find ourselves engaging in an icebreaking exercise that feels like a blowtorch to the skin. I sense, without turning to look, that Stacy is somewhere behind me, writhing inwardly as she murmurs this mantra into the eyes of another stranger. As I meet Peter's gaze, I can sense his surface terror at this disorienting public intimacy doing battle with something deeper: the softening grief that has propelled him through his reservations to a roomful of metal folding chairs and stricken strangers.

The exercise ends. I drop Peter's hands, he drops mine, and we behold each other for a brief moment. The icebreaking exercise worked: we have fight-or-flight hormones coursing through our systems, and we see each other more sharply, the way animals see rustling in the bushes right before they're eaten.

"If everybody could please take your seats again?" calls the seminar leader.

I turn from Peter to Stacy, who stands behind me looking shaken. She inquires with her eyes and I answer with mine: **Yes, I'm OK. That was fucked, but I'm OK.** She nods slightly, agreeing. We both resume our spots in the two folding chairs in the last row nearest the door.

We have chosen these seats strategically, in accordance with our one rule: if one of us feels uncomfortable or is seized by an emotion too unpleasant to get a grip on, we will nudge the other (we have a safe word) and leave. We are not "group" people by nature, a quality we passed on to Greta: when I once took her to a neighborhood sing-along, her little hand gripped my shoulder as the other kids ran up eagerly to the woman leading it, wiggling and clapping. I could hear her unspoken question: **Daddy, what are all these people** doing?

It is November; Greta has been dead six months. I think of her discomfort as I glance around the room: What **are** we doing? There are about sixty of us here at the Kripalu Institute in Stockbridge, Massachusetts, about three hours north of New York City up the Taconic State Parkway. Some have lost older children—drug overdoses, suicides, car accidents—and some have lost spouses, mothers, fathers. We all share one thing in common: something happened to us that is supposed to only happen to other people. We have all been pushed here, jostled into position—by life, by circumstance, by scheduling, and, finally, by the seminar leader himself, who has moved us next to one another like school-children. The grief has taken control of a number of things we once thought were ours.

This seminar is called "From Grieving to

Believing," and neither Stacy nor I can quite say the name aloud without wincing. It is led by David Kessler, a thanatologist and grief expert who has written books with Elisabeth Kübler-Ross, she of the hallowed five stages and sort of a secular saint of Western grieving.

There are two other retreat leaders besides Kessler, here to attend to various states of our emotional and metaphysical distress. One of them is a yoga teacher named Paul Denniston, who specializes in something called "grief yoga," which we practice every morning before breakfast, in a room full of sobs, some stifled, many open. The other is a medium named Maureen Hancock.

It was the presence of Maureen that Stacy and I circled back to, over and over again, in the car on the way up. What would she **do**? Our level of familiarity and comfort with the idea of a medium went about as far as Whoopi Goldberg's pink pillbox hat and rolled-back eyes in **Ghost**. Ludicrous scenarios proliferated in our heads, and we joked: Would she speak in tongues? Would she fall to the floor and begin to thrash? Behind our dumb jokes, we nursed the unvoiced worry: What had our grief made of us? Had we now joined ranks with the suckers, the wide-eyed, the willfully deluded?

But we didn't say any of this, probably because we heard how sour and uncharitable it sounded even in our heads. Instead, there in the car, we nervously repeated the same promise to each other every half hour or so. "Look, this might be weird," one of us would say. "But if one of us hates it, we can just leave! We don't have to be there. We're doing this only because we want to. We can just leave."

It becomes clear to us only a few moments after arriving at the seminar that our exit plan is nonviable. "I just have one rule," says Kessler. "If you feel like you need to leave, you have to tell me. Everyone in this room has had someone in their lives disappear, so no one can just walk out without saying anything first."

Stacy and I look at each other: **Fuck.**

Kessler wears a collared shirt beneath a snug baby-blue sweater suited for the soft white lights of daytime TV. A tiny headset microphone peeks discreetly out at the left corner of his mouth, and he paces before us like we are his living room furniture. His voice is high and soft and soothing, and his words are beveled smooth and polished into gleaming slogans: "Grief is a reflection of a connection that has been lost," he says, with the slight loping cadence you adopt when you've repeated something a thousand times. "It is a reflection of that love you had for that individual."

Behind him, a PowerPoint presentation fires up. On it, I see my life whittled remorselessly into the neat bullet points of the five stages: denial, anger, bargaining, depression, acceptance. One of them says, curiously, "Arguing with the Snow."

Walking in front of the projector light, so his passing shadow bulges on the screen, Kessler asks us, "What if it were snowing outside right now, and I was standing outside, enraged? Imagine you walked past me on the way in, and I was pointing at the snow on the ground as it fell, and I was yelling, 'You're not supposed to be here! It is not supposed to be snowing! I don't like snow! Don't be here!'"

He pauses for a few snickers. "What would you say? You would say, 'Oh my god, there's

a crazy person outside arguing with reality.'
You would say, 'David, **it's snowing;** it snowed
yesterday. You're **arguing with the snow.**'"

He stops pacing at this, does a quick heel
turn, and pans across the room. "That's what
I try to tell people when they refuse to own
their own reality. I try and tell them, 'You are
arguing with the snow.' In other words, you
can have your own opinions all you want, but
reality is gonna win.

"One of the main things I don't think
people realize is that a broken heart is an open
heart," he continues. "It's a heart that's open,
that can be healed, can be changed, can be
re-formed, can grow new patterns for new
types of love. One of the things I want us to
work on is to begin to find ways to take that
broken heart and allow it to feel that pain,
but to grow."

Grief is healing, healing is grief—these
blandishments soothe me like a warm com-
press to my forehead. As he speaks, I feel
my need for complicating thoughts—for
complex ideas with fancy conditional hinges
that swing open onto interpretations—being
scrubbed clean. Sniffles have already broken

out in the audience: an ambient noise that will continue through the weekend. At the end of each row, boxes of tissues—cheap ones, harsh and nose chafing—sit like votive candles. They are passed down from the end of the row to the middle as needed.

"Grief is fluid, and it is always changing," he reminds us. "The writer Anne Lamott once said that your brain is a bad neighborhood, and you should never go into it alone." Above all, "grief is as unique as a fingerprint. We can show you the stages, but they are not a linear journey. In the end, nothing and no one can hand you the map to your own grief."

The session lasts an hour and a half, and when it is done, he says, "OK, now go get some lunch and come back ready for Maureen, who is going to do some very exciting work with you."

✧

After lunch, Stacy and I have a few minutes to kill before Maureen begins. We wander around downstairs, passing signs for a writers' workshop called "Writing Down the Light" and for an upcoming seminar called "Facing Cancer with Courage." David Kessler's books occupy a whole corner shelf of the bookstore to the left. Across the hall, a café with windows looking out onto the grounds sells iced coffee, ice-cream bars, and other worldly pleasures. People sit around, scrolling through their phones, talking loudly without looking up.

We file back into the studio a few minutes before the second session is supposed to begin. A trimly built middle-aged man with close-cropped silver hair enters alongside us, nodding absently in our direction. We smile nervously; the code of social conduct is muddy in a roomful of bereaved strangers. We all know at least one intimate thing about one another, with zero knowledge of the details. It is a little like attending a family reunion with only the second cousins whose names you don't remember.

A young-looking couple takes their seats behind us, and I glance back at them. I wonder what manner of loss brought them here. Something in their demeanor suggests to me we have something awful in common. They are haggard, drawn, depleted looking, despite being fiercely fit. I study them more closely for signs of "dead child." The man gazes around, examining others and then smiling furtively and looking away when he accidentally makes eye contact. The woman stares straight ahead at nothing.

In front, Maureen grabs the microphone and strides out, all business and instant chatter. She reminds me of some brassy comedian from the late '80s, pacing the room at twice the speed of Kessler and spitting rapid-fire patter in a flat Boston Irish accent.

"As a little kid, I used to see spirits walking all around the house," she says. "We're Irish, my parents had a lot of parties; I thought they were drunken house guests!" Some laughs break out. "I tell ya, it's not easy sometimes," she continues. "It's a little hard to ride the subway and have a spirit elbow you, saying, 'Hey, scooch over! You're sitting next to my grandson, and I got a few things to tell him.' One day I was at the drugstore, just trying to buy a hairbrush, and the checkout clerk's sister wouldn't leave me alone, she was just jumping up and down. Finally I had to look over my shoulder and snap, 'Will you keep your pants on for a second? I just need to buy a gosh-darn hairbrush.' There was no one there! I turn around and the woman behind the counter is looking at me like I'm the Exorcist."

She's not **funny**, exactly, but she is exuberant and warm, and the room lightens with her energy. People are laughing. She stops pacing, smiles at us. "You see, sometimes I come out and I come on a little strong, and people are like, 'Aye, what's the story with this broad?'" she acknowledges. "But I'm trying to get your energy up! Laughing, crying, all of those activities help bring our energies up, and that helps me tune in to you."

She stops her monologue and closes her eyes, fanning herself gently with one hand. "OK, I'm getting something here," she announces, eyes still shut.

I glance over at Stacy out of the corner of my eye and notice that she's leaning forward slightly. My body is taut.

"Did somebody over here . . . somebody over here . . ." Maureen wanders down the middle aisle, passing the first five rows of chairs. She is three folding chairs ahead of us. Every head turns slightly to follow her. She stops.

"I'm seeing a wife," she announces. "She died of cancer. She died of cancer, and it's been a few years." Her eyes are still closed, and a smile flickers across her face: "Oh wow, she's got a really big energy." Her eyes open, unfocused, and she says carefully, as if reciting, "Tell Marie that she has to finish college." She looks around: "Does that mean anything to anybody?"

The trim middle-aged man who entered the room with us is sitting right in front of her, and he raises his hand. "That's my wife," he says, clearly and calmly. "Lorraine. She died two years ago."

"Ah, ah," Maureen says, excited and coming up to him. "What's your name, sir?"

"My name is Philip, and my daughter is Marie," Philip says. "She's been having trouble ever since her mom passed, and she's been talking about taking a year off college. I've been trying to convince her to stay."

There are murmurs in the room. Stacy and I make eye contact again: **Holy shit.**

Maureen invites Philip up to the front of the room, and he takes a seat on a stool in front of the projector screen. Maureen sits very close, her body facing his, and reaches out to clasp one hand. She's still holding the microphone with the other hand. "This isn't the first time she's reached out to you since she passed on, is it?" she asks.

Philip shakes his head gravely: **No, it is not.** "Last Thanksgiving, we were all sitting around the table, all the kids and the family friends," he says, "and then the weirdest thing happened—all of the lights flickered on and off in the house. The power hadn't gone out, because the stove and the microwave were still working. We all looked around at each other to make sure we were seeing the same thing."

Maureen's smile broadens and she closes her eyes again, deeply satisfied. "That was her," she says, "that was her. Was it a memory of something? She's saying, 'Last Christmas! Last Christmas!'"

Again, Philip nods smoothly. "Yes, it was," he confirms. "She's talking about the last time we were all together as a family. It was

Christmas, and the lights went out while we were all at dinner."

Philip isn't overcome with emotion from any of this. His voice is deep and clear, his skin browned as if he lives somewhere where he spends most of his time outdoors. His shoulders are relaxed, his posture straight, even sitting on the stool. The intimacy of Maureen's touch, the attention of the entire room, the contemplation of his wife reaching out to him from the beyond—all of it seems to be exactly as he already knew it to be, and Maureen has simply confirmed it. He is serene.

The sniffling has broken out again. I steal a glance at the young couple behind me. The man is looking straight down at his hands, and the woman seems to have drawn further inside herself. Her temples are slightly recessed, and her hazel eyes are completely opaque.

Up in front, Lorraine is still insisting via Maureen that her daughter finish college. "She won't let that go, she's practically tugging on my shoulder," Maureen says. " 'Make sure! Make sure she promises to finish school.' "

She playfully socks him in the arm and says, "Wow, she could be a bossy lady, huh?"

Philip smiles at this, deepening new lines in his face. He is stoic, but his voice warms: "Yes, ma'am," he says simply. "She sure could."

"Well, you two loved each other more than anything, that's very obvious to me," Maureen says. "God bless you, and God bless your family." She hugs Philip and sends him back to his seat as people start clapping.

The room feels different now. An assortment of strangers has been united in a tidal wave of mutual need, and the need is pure enough that we are suddenly unconcerned about how we appear to others. There are no more nameless "suckers" in here, and there are no skeptics. Stacy and I turn to look at each other; I try to raise a **how about that?** eyebrow, but I can feel that my face is white. The woman at the end of our row, wearing sweats, stands up abruptly, folds her leg beneath her, and sits back down on it, crossing her arms tightly over her chest.

Maureen has closed her eyes again, and I can see her eyes flutter slightly beneath the lids. There is another pause as we wait. "I am seeing a lot of tattoos," she says. "A guy, a young guy, he has tattoos all up and down his arms." Then, "Oh man, he's got a very **new** energy, and he's talking so fast I can't get him to calm down. He's jumping up and down. He keeps shouting, 'There he is! There he is! Right there in the back!'" She opens her eyes. "Is there someone whose name starts with 'P' back there? I'm getting the letter 'P.' P . . . Peter? Is there a Peter?"

I immediately twist in my chair to find my partner in the icebreaking exercise rigid with fear. Slowly, as if unbidden, his long left arm rises. Maureen sweeps down past us, around to his corner chair in the back. Everyone in the front rows turns on their chairs to follow her. The seminar wallflowers are now center stage.

Peter is more than six feet tall, and he looks supremely uncomfortable on his steel-grey folding chair, his knees at acute angles and his legs splayed. But he does not stand as Maureen waits over him. He just looks up at her like she's a flight attendant offering him ginger ale. Maureen will not allow this.

"Well, come on, get up, get up!" she says,

reaching down and clasping his shoulder. "I'm not gonna crouch down there."

Slowly, painfully, he unfolds himself, presents himself to the room.

"I sense this is a loved one, and he was close in age to you," she says, then asks, "How old are you?"

Peter speaks without leaning his head toward the microphone, just loud enough for me to hear him: "I'm twenty-eight."

"OK, and he's a few years older?" Maureen asks. Peter nods. "Is he a cousin or a . . . brother?"

"He was my brother," states Peter, looking up and making eye contact. His voice is clearer when he says this.

Maureen's eyes and voice soften. "He just crossed over recently, didn't he?" She pauses again, and then lower, "It was drugs, wasn't it?"

Peter stiffens slightly but holds her eyes. "Heroin," he says quietly.

"Ah," she says. Then: "When did he pass?"

"Two weeks ago," Peter says.

"Oh my god," the woman sitting next to me in sweatpants says under her breath.

I want to get up, to hug Peter, or at least, since he would hate that, to shield him from the glare of the room, to put him somewhere comfortable where he will not have to endure the stares of strangers. I ache for him in my seat.

"He wants you to know he's fine," Maureen assures him. "He just keeps saying, 'I know I fucked up, buddy, I know I fucked up.' He had been clean for a while?"

Peter nods again, says nothing.

" 'Take care of Mom,' he is saying over and over again. He says it was an accident, he didn't mean to do it, he's sorry. He loves you."

Peter is looking right at her now, and his back has straightened.

"He's just like a big border collie." Maureen laughs. "So you were the younger one, but you were always kind of taking care of him. Is that right?"

A small smile tugs at Peter: "That's right."

"Yeah," Maureen says, simply and fondly, "yeah.

" 'I'm fine, tell him I'm fine,' he keeps saying that," she repeats. "And he says, 'Thank you.' That's coming through really loud and really clear. 'Thank you.'" She regards Peter tenderly. "You are a really good brother to him, and that's never gonna change," she says. "He loves you. He wants you to relax." She mimics grabbing his shoulders and shaking him playfully and says, "Hey, buddy, loosen up!"

Peter flinches slightly at the contact but relaxes into it.

"He was always telling you that, huh?" she says.

At this, Peter actually grins. "Yeah," he admits.

"Oh, how wonderful. You're wonderful, your brother is wonderful. Give me a hug," Maureen gushes, and the room claps again, more loudly this time.

Stacy and I find ourselves, as the session goes on, aching to be chosen. **Pick me,** we plead silently. **Greta, we are here. Greta, come get Mommy and Daddy.** Maureen jokes about how many spirits are crowding in line, raising their hands, asking to be picked.

"I think maybe there are too many adults here for Greta to get through," Stacy whispers to me.

I picture our daughter, standing next to

me at a birthday party, watching the merri-
ment warily with one hand on her mommy's
shoulder, straining her neck to peek over the
scrum. She would have no chance in a room
like this, I think. I know where I would find
her: in the back, watching the room, taking
everything in. The session ends with no word
from her, and as people file out, Stacy and I
sit, unwilling to move.

✧

As you move up in Kripalu's three-floor
compound, you ascend out of worldliness:
upstairs, phones are not allowed. The breakfast in the main cafeteria is meant to be taken
in silence. We discover this latter bit the following morning, as we navigate the cafeteria's
funereal atmosphere, utterly silent save for the
clinks of forks and the sips of tea. I carry my
tray, deeply conscious of the rattle and movement of my silverware and plate on it.

Ahead of me, Stacy picks a brown mug
from an inverted stack and moves to fill it
before wheeling on me, her eyes popping,
hissing in a stage whisper that carries across

the room like a megaphone: "**Oh my god,
they don't have any fucking coffee!**"

I shush her frantically, waving my arms
like I'm fanning a fire. No heads turn, but
I feel the heat of interested eyes swiveling.
Still grumbling, she follows me to the end
of a crowded table, where we sit. A woman
with a small Bible is at my elbow, raising bites
of organic granola with sunflower seeds to her
mouth as she reads.

"I think they make it silent so no one
has a riot about the goddamn coffee," Stacy
grumbles sotto voce as we walk out. We spend
the following two mornings in the first-floor
café, drinking strong coffee, scrolling through
Facebook, and enjoying the company of our
kind: the ambivalent, the uncertain, the
dabblers.

Sickeningly, it turns out I was right about
the young couple: Kevin and Melissa, married seven years. They lost their youngest
daughter, Callie, two years ago, when she
was four years old. There was no accident, no
sickness; she simply went to bed one night
and never woke up. The autopsy revealed
nothing. "When I came in the next morning,

she was just gone," Melissa says, shrugging almost apologetically.

We are eating lunch together after the second day's morning session, near a window that looks out onto fields. I understand her body language, the instinctive mea culpa for not being able to offer a more meaningful account. Kevin picks at a plate of quinoa and spinach, staring down at it. He smiles wanly in acknowledgment of the story's inadequacy.

"It was just so hard to explain to everyone— our family, the kids at her preschool," Melissa says. "She wasn't sick. Nothing happened to her. It's already hard enough to explain to other kids when kids die. With Callie, there wasn't even a reason. I just felt like the worst mom in the world."

"How did the other parents explain to their kids?" I ask. I remember Greta's best friend, Eva, had looked at us with an almost religious fear: we ran into Eva and her mom on the street one day, about ten days after, and she hid behind her mother's legs. "It's OK, Eva, Greta's in the sky now," her mother said helplessly, trying and failing to extricate her. From behind her mother, Eva's brown eyes pierced mine, accusatory and focused: her best friend was suddenly gone and we were still standing, and the only conclusion she could reach was that we had done something heinous to her.

Stacy and I had walked back to our building in grim silence. We felt like monsters, Gorgons sent to terrify the fortunate. Behind us, I envisioned cars veering slowly into fire hydrants, flowers shriveling, store windows shattering, old ladies clutching their hearts and collapsing as their pacemakers malfunctioned in our wake.

"Some of our friends stopped talking to us after a while," Melissa acknowledges when we tell her this story. "It's just too hard for them to imagine; it's so hard for **us** to imagine. No one should have to imagine it. After a while, they were just too spooked to see us again."

"Yeah," Stacy agrees. "It's just too much for a lot of people. I don't blame anyone for it. It's too much for us, too." Stacy and I don't say it, but we both feel a rush of gratitude for our friend circle, which activated around us immediately. No one flinched when they looked us in the eyes, and all our loved ones seemed to know exactly what to say. No one left us alone, and almost no one overstayed their welcome. I sopped up all this love greedily, eagerly, like I was pressing a bread crust into a corner of a soup dish. Most days it was the only evidence I had of Greta's life, that I had ever been her father.

Melissa and Kevin are the first couple we've met who have lost a toddler, and there is a ghastly sort of relief in it. A pall of societal shame hovers over everyone in this club, the haunted inverse of new-parent meet-ups and mommy groups. Children who lose parents are orphans; bereaved spouses are widows. But what do you call parents who lose children? It seems telling to me there is no word in our language for our situation. It is unspeakable, and by extension, we are not supposed to exist.

"It feels like I'm closeted and trying to figure out if someone I'm talking to is gay," Stacy observes of the furtive effort to find community. While I grapple with anger, Stacy has grappled with loneliness: Where are the others? Stacy's world-map coordinates consist entirely of trustworthy people, nodes of conversation, repositories of wisdom, sources of support. She seeks out and builds these social networks effortlessly, like a spider spins silk.

Give anyone five minutes with Stacy, even the most private soul, and she will gently prod them open with the force of her genuine curiosity. Surface questions—"What do you do for a living?"—yield instantly to the richer stuff: what they think about their job, what else they might have done if they'd had the courage, the sorts of friends they wished they'd made, their thoughts on free will. She is charismatic in the purest sense: there is nothing sinister or needful lurking beneath it, no raw deal being struck. She simply wants to know about you.

But building this particular group has eluded even Stacy. Some googling turns up support groups for women who have miscarried or for parents of deceased older kids—teenagers who have overdosed, died in a car accident, committed suicide, or died of cancer. But locating other young parents who have had their toddlers struck down, in all their babbling, rude health, is nearly impossible. We are vigilant about not succumbing to self-pity the way we are vigilant about flossing daily, and yet sometimes our situation practically begs it of us. Our inability to find a single family anywhere in our circumstances feels like just such an invitation. Sometimes I see self-pity running up to me like a neighborhood dog, flopping on its back and showing me its belly. **Come on, indulge,** it says.

"I was grateful that there was at least no single person for us to blame, really," Stacy says. "And that there was no . . . **ambiguity** about it. We didn't have to make any really hard decisions. It was pretty clear-cut that she wasn't going to survive."

"Having no one to blame was the hardest part about Callie," Melissa says. "You doubt yourself. Even though there was nothing you did. You just can't help it. I asked myself a million questions about the night before. Did I miss something? Were we not paying attention? But there was just nothing. It makes the anger . . . difficult."

"Yeah, I mean, who do we have to be angry at?" I wonder out loud. "It was a goddamn building that killed her. How can I be mad at a building?"

"Jayson's had a lot more of the anger," Stacy says. "I've just had . . . I don't know." She flicks her eyes down, suddenly overwhelmed. I seek out Kevin's eyes, wondering if the anger is a fundamentally male thing. Kevin meets my eyes, but his are glassy and inward. He has the air of the only non-English speaker in a group, marooned in a room of incomprehensible babble. All he can offer is a bland smile, a helpless sort of shrug.

"We went back to work too soon," Stacy says. "We kind of needed it at the time, but now we are really wishing we had more time away."

"Yeah, I remember all I wanted to do after Callie died was to go to India," Melissa says. "If I could have, I would have just gone to an ashram for a year. It was hard, though, having an older kid. We had to take care of him, so we didn't really get to process a lot of things. Nolan really needed us, and he was confused, too."

The evening before, we were asked to

write letters to our loved ones, and Melissa and Stacy commiserate over the difficulty of the exercise. "It's hard to know what to say to her," says Stacy. "She talked a lot for a two-year-old, we were really lucky she was so verbal, but still, the things she liked were . . . noodles. Chocolate. She really liked **Frozen.**"

"We were going to bring Callie to see **Frozen,**" Melissa remembers. "We watched the preview together on the computer. She died a few months before it came out."

"Oh god," I say. "Did you ever see it?"

"We did," she says. "We went to the movies to see it that December, and I blubbered the whole way through."

✧

Keeping with our noncommittal, half-measures approach, we've chosen not to stay on Kripalu grounds, driving just another mile and a half down the road to a randomly chosen B&B. We've justified this decision by the exorbitant price of the private rooms there, but truthfully, we are just afraid of feel-ing trapped.

Last night we lay next to each other on our floral four-poster bed in silence. We held our phones, and after a hesitant moment, we each began typing silently. Even typing "Greta" as an address, with a comma, brought with it a sharp pain. "Greta" has been an absence, the hole that sucked all the sound from our lives, and we have until now been mostly content to move under its woolly silence. To openly address her, to turn up the volume on that absence with no intermediaries or buffers, felt palpably dangerous, even illicit, like an exorcism.

"Hi, sweetie," I started. "Daddy and Mommy want to be OK for you, because you loved us happy. We are here because there are other people who are sad, too, who miss their mommy or their daddy or friend or brother or sister, or even their little boy or girl like you."

Tears muddled my vision. I glanced over and saw Stacy crying silently as well, her eyes red and cheeks pink. I turned back to my phone and felt a pain in the hollow of my bones. I squeezed my eyes shut for a second to eject the tears rolling down my cheeks and puddling at my collar. Then I continued.

"Oh, sweetie pie," I wrote. "We miss you every day. We miss you every morning when you don't wake us up and every night when we don't get to kiss you good night." The memories snowballed; I began tapping faster, and my letter became simply a moan, a long list of things we didn't do together anymore: play with blocks on the floor, point at pictures in books. After a few sentences, I felt I was talking to myself, to my self-pity and my loneliness, which had filled the shape left by her absence. Before I could even stop to look, I was staring at five paragraphs. My last sentence was simple: "I remember how it felt to be parents."

When we were done, we switched phones. Stacy's was two paragraphs long. "Sometimes I'm afraid to address you, sweetie, and I don't know why," it said at one point. "It's so hard not having you here, knowing all the things we never got to experience with you, left wondering who you would have become." It ended, heartbreakingly, with "I miss you every day, Greta. I'm sorry." I caught my breath slightly at this: "I'm sorry."

I snuck a look at Stacy's face out of the

corner of my eye: Did she live, silently, with blame? I wondered about this. Stacy was Greta's mother long before I was Greta's father. She carried Greta, talked to her under her breath as she swam inside her. The two of them understood each other on a level that surpassed language.

I flashed back on Greta's birth for a moment, the indescribable and awe-inspiring teamwork between them that I witnessed. As Greta was crowning, she was facedown. Each push brought her small, mottled purple head briefly into view, more internal organ than person. Then she receded, a movement from nothingness into fullness and back again. "Her heart rate is gorgeous," our midwife, Rita, informed us, monitoring with a hand-held device and a matter-of-fact tone.

Stacy's hand clutched my hair, a fistful, as each contraction hit. She opened up from socialized moans and deep breaths into primitive stuff: guttural screaming, the sound of your genetic inheritance claiming control.

The next contraction arrived, Stacy's hand re-clenched the clump of hair it held, my skull went numb-tingling hot, and Greta's head resurfaced, hanging there. Then, so surreal that I never once quite believe it after I see it, I watched it rotate, 180 degrees, so she was facing up; I could confirm it was happening only by watching the tiny bits of hair on her head as a reference point. I lay back on my side to be even with Stacy's face to tell her what had happened; with her eyes closed, concentrating somewhere deeper than all of us, she smiled. Then her eyebrows knitted again, and she whispered loudly, fiercely, **"She's coming."** Then there was another push, maybe two, before Stacy reached down in between her legs and pulled Greta up.

"Hi, beautiful," Stacy breathed to her, grey and shaky. Greta, wailing, promptly pooped all over her mother's chest, covering both of them in tarry-black meconium that her small feet swiped through feebly like a bird trapped in an oil slick.

Behind us, I heard Rita's voice losing some of its loose California sunniness: "Mom is bleeding a little bit," she said. There was a medical bustle I didn't watch, a clink of some instruments I didn't see. Greta's arms were in a T shape, doing the primitive, helpless shake of all new humans. Stacy patted her, whispering, "Shh, shh." At one point, I glanced down at Rita, to see what she was doing, and I still have a vivid, dreamlike memory of her: she is wearing a headlamp, and in her left gloved hand she holds a needle, pulling one long clear thread up from somewhere inside Stacy I don't care to observe.

As she lost blood, Stacy's arms started to shake a little harder, so Greta, still wailing, was passed off to me. I placed her tiny body on my left shoulder and sang "Between the Bars" into her ear to her for the first time; her crying broke up and then subsided.

A few hours later, the blood all over the bed was removed in one lump, sheets and pads and all, and dumped in a large biohazard bucket in the corner of our room. A nurse placed a clear bassinet next to our bed and swaddled Greta with the expertise of soldiers folding a flag at an army funeral, placing her inside. The second she left to let us sleep, we scooped Greta out quietly, placing her in the bed between us. We watched as her bird-like breastbone rose and fell. Stacy gazed at her in fond recognition. She said it again, her face radiant, transformed by a smile: "Hi, beautiful." These two, I realized, knew each other. They had passed through life's messiest trial, working and breathing together.

Did Stacy, as Greta's original caretaker, the body that carried Greta's body, carry some original-sin sense of guilt? I remembered talking to Elizabeth months after her daughter, Clara, was born, as she fought through the fog of postpartum depression: "It's like seeing someone hold one of my internal organs, or my left arm," she commented of seeing others hold Clara. It is common enough for parents of children who die to say that "a piece" of them has died, but reading Stacy's note, I thought again how literal it was for her, how figurative for me. "I'm sorry."

At lunch with Kevin and Melissa, I glance at them and I wonder which of them is carrying their letters. I wonder if only Melissa wrote one, or if she put pen to paper and found that she couldn't say a word. Maybe Kevin pounded away on his phone's keyboard, screaming soundlessly in perfect ten-point

font. I take a sip of hot herbal tea and cradle
the mug, thinking how strange it is that we
are four adults out to lunch, each of us with
a letter to our dead child somewhere on our
person.

We walk back from the cafeteria to the
studio together, Stacy and Melissa up ahead
chatting and Kevin and I hanging back
together, mostly silent. When we take our
seats, I catch sight of Stacy's eyes, and I spot
something new in them: a light, however
wan. When Stacy is sad, her eyes turn murky,
like steely harbor water at night. Now it is as
if someone has dropped a pin light into that
water, something that sank and disappeared
fast but not before sending a faint signal to
the surface.

✧

"I hope you all had a nice break," David
Kessler says to us when everyone has settled
in for our afternoon session. "If you remember, yesterday at the end of our session I asked
you to write a letter to your loved one. Did we
all write the letter?"

There is a general murmur of assent.

"Does everyone here have their letter? OK, great, why don't you get those out now?"

I look around the room, which is suddenly abuzz with rustling and digging. Sitting in front of us, I see Melissa gripping the edges of a sheet of yellow legal paper she has produced from her bag and unfolded. Her entire body is taut, and the edges of her fingers are white. I catch sight of red pen scrawl on it and avert my eyes before any of the letters resolve themselves into words. I feel unclean for even glancing at it.

"Who would like to read theirs?" Kessler asks.

Stacy jabs me slightly with her elbow; she knows I quietly burn for this sort of visibility, need it. I tend to stand up straighter in the spotlight, where she shrinks from it instinctively; she spent the majority of our wedding reception in a state of near-total panic, unable to join a group without producing an uproar.

I raise my hand, slowly, as if I am still debating the action as it happens. Kessler's eyes alight on me, and I feel the room's energy shift with him. He is a master communicator and

controller of the room, so practiced at corral-
ling and directing the emotions of a group of
brokenhearted people that there doesn't seem
to be anything high-stakes about the work
at all. "Yes, you right there," he calls. "Why
don't you read us what you wrote? First, tell
us a little bit about who the letter is to."

I clear my throat.

"It is to our daughter," I say, my voice
emerging a little squeaky and then dropping
too deep.

"I'm sorry," Kessler says, keeping his eyes
locked on mine. I feel a bit like I have taken
hostages somewhere and Kessler has been
dispatched to talk me down. I sense everyone
glancing at me and at Stacy. I focus my eyes,
already burning, on my phone and begin
to read.

When I hit the middle of the letter—"We
have a picture of your mama holding you,
wearing her sun hat and sitting on a tree
stump. I feel like you got to have eight good
days with your family where you knew what
life could be, how much fun you and your
daddy were going to have together, and then
you were taken from us"—I start to hear small

noises of grief, small murmurs and "ohs" and tissues rasping out of cheap boxes.

When I finish, I look up and find Kessler regarding us gravely. "How old was your daughter when she died?" he asks me.

"She was two," I tell him, surprised by the ripples of shock that pass through the room; we have heard already from people whose adult children have hanged themselves, who have died as teenagers from cancer.

"Was she ill?" Kessler asks, and I feel that familiar anticipatory messenger's dread.

"No. A brick fell from the eighth story of a building and hit her."

I hear gasps. From the corner of my eye, I see that dog of self-pity, trotting up near me and wagging its tail: **Even in this room, with these people, you're still a rock star of grief,** it says, cocking an eyebrow. **Even these shattered people can't imagine being you. How about** that?

"That is a terrible story, and I am sorry to learn it," Kessler says. He pauses, then adds, "You sound angry. Are you angry?"

"Yes," I say, and I feel the dangerous heat come out of my voice, pulling tears with it.

"I'm angry all the time now. I never used to be. I've always **hated** anger. Everything bad I'd ever seen happen in my life was because someone was angry at someone else. Anger makes people hurt each other. I didn't want anger in my heart. Now I live with it constantly. I feel like I am going to choke on it." I am crying now. "I feel like less of a human. I feel like I have cancer."

"Of course you are angry," Kessler says. "I am angry for you just hearing this story. Could you both do me a favor, please? I'd like you to come up to the front of the room."

I glance over at Stacy to read her eyes, which have gone opaque with panic. Thanks to me, we are entering her worst nightmare in slow motion. Asking Stacy to "please come up to the front of the room" is a bit like inviting an ant to please step underneath this magnifying glass, or to please willfully place your hand into this wood chipper. We slowly stand and file our way through the center of the rows of folding chairs.

"I'd like to do some anger work," Kessler says. "We have all these ideas about anger in our society—that it's bad, that it's dangerous, that we should suppress it. It's natural to be angry, and frankly it's healthy. We feel anger **for a good reason**, and it only makes us feel sick or lash out when we deny it and fail to let it loose into the world."

He turns to me. "Jayson, you said that you thought anger hurt people, and I don't think that's true. I think suppressed anger hurts people. I think anger is a positive emotion, and we only truly let go of it when we honor it."

He has cleared some space in the front of the room, and he bounds over to the corner, where there are yoga props, returning with two fat, soft rectangular support pillows and handing them to us. "Pounding pillows is a classic technique for releasing anger," he says. "Here's what I want you to do; actually, here, I'll show you." With that, he leaps down to his knees with startling alacrity, and he raises both of his fists above his head like a comic-book villain cursing the heavens and brings them down, rhythmically, as he screams: "IT JUST! ISN'T! FAIR!"

I catch Stacy's eyes again, which have widened further as the scope of our exposure becomes clear. Kessler jumps back up, dust-ing off his knees, and holds out the pillow, expectant: "Here. Here you go. Go on!"

This has gone beyond Stacy's worst night-mare into absurdist territory. My throat is constricting with guilt, but the laws of group dynamics are working, and the two of us kneel, slowly and queasily, on the small wooden pallet that sits in front of the room. There are blankets folded over double to cushion our knees. Then we look up at him helplessly, like children awaiting instructions from a kindergarten teacher.

"OK, now I want you to think of some-thing to say," he says. "What makes you angry? What do you hate?"

I think for a second. "I hate happy families," I tell him. "Whenever I see a family taking a walk, or a father with a child on his shoulders, all I can feel is rage and hatred. I hate them. Sometimes I actually wish something terrible will happen to them, and then I feel nause-ated; how did this get inside of me?"

"Well, what right do they have, to have a child when you've lost yours?" Kessler shouts. "I want you to say it now, and hit the pillow as you say it: 'I hate happy families!' And for support, we're all going to say it with you. Ready? One . . . two . . . three!"

The walls nearly shake as the crowd shouts along with me, but I might as well be alone for all I notice it. "I hate happy families!" I scream, slamming my hands into the softness, feeling them sink.

As I pound, I feel currents loose themselves in me. Violence, I sense, has been lurking inside of me. I slam and howl in a roomful of adults, and as I do, a buried dream—one I've had more than once but haven't allowed to dislodge from the lowest rungs of my subconscious—bubbles up.

In the dream, my anger becomes a person—a man, midthirties and white like me, nondescript. He is probably a composite of all the healthy, rested, and contented men I pass on my morning commute. In the dream, I find myself doing profound, monstrous violence to that person. I kneel on this protesting man's chest, my knees cutting off his airway and his face turning beet red, his eyes pleading with mine as he splutters. Rearing up deliberately, I hit him, hard, in the nose and feel the thin bones give way instantly, crunching into softer viscera beneath. I hear him scream, hear liquid fill his mouth and turn his cries wet. I pound and I pound. My fists glisten. The face below me becomes unrecognizable. In my dream, I let out a war-like scream, as if to notify the world around me: it cannot take from me and expect me to remain mute.

I am slamming the pillow repeatedly with both fists now. I sense Stacy is somewhere behind me. She hovers over her pillow, her hands curled into reluctant half-fists, a passenger on a journey I have signed us up for.

"Stacy, what are you angry at?" Kessler demands.

She looks stricken. "I don't know," she says.

"Well, come on!" Kessler says, goading her. "Your daughter was killed! What kind of world do we live in that would allow that to happen?"

Even with blood racing in my temples, I tense and turn around, snapping instinctively at Kessler: "Don't YELL at her!"

"Well, the building was a center for seniors, and now when I walk around, I feel . . .

sometimes, when I walk past older people, I have a hard time . . ."

She falters, and my throat constricts. I feel like I am watching her thoughts withdraw into her preverbal cortex like a tape measure zipping shut.

She takes a breath. "They just . . . they make me angry sometimes. But what am I supposed to do? I can't go around saying 'I hate old people,'" she says, letting out a nervous little laugh.

"Sure you can!" Kessler cries, pouncing on the line. "You **absolutely** can. Everyone here knows what that means. You don't really hate old people. You hate the time that they have; you hate that they have lived full lives while Greta's was cut short. Everyone is going to join with you now; why don't you pound the pillow and scream 'I hate old people!'"

Stacy's eyes widen in horror.

"Are you ready?" he demands, and then counts, "One . . . two . . . three . . . I HATE OLD PEOPLE!"

I look at the room and see a silver-haired woman in the front row, holding a pillow and screaming along. "I hate old people!"

she hollers, the corners of her mouth turned up ever so slightly. Some, unable to help themselves, laugh. I do, too, even as I kneel like a penitent on the floor in front of them. We have become some sort of infernal rally, mobilizing to stick it to all those old people and happy families. My hands are warm, and my face flushes with pleasure.

"You see the power anger can have," Kessler observes. "When we stop to release it, and to feel it, it can set us free. Now, I'd like to thank Stacy and Jayson for being so brave. If anyone else wants to follow their example, I'd like to invite everyone to grab a pillow and take a seat anywhere they would like on the floor. Everyone is free to shout whatever they want, at whatever time; the important thing is that you get it out of your system."

I watch in wonder as nearly all the chairs empty, and men and women station themselves in corners. Two women come up to the front and plop their pillows directly in front of us, on the wooden raised pallet.

"OK, is everyone ready?" Kessler calls. "On the count of three, I'm going to ask everyone to just let go of everything they have. Put all of your anger into that pillow, and shout whatever comes to your mind. OK? One . . . two . . . three!"

The room erupts. In the far left corner, a stocky, intense man begins screaming about his in-laws. I can't make out if his dead loved one is a son or his wife. A woman next to him wails and pounds as she rails against her dead mother for leaving her with her sister. "I've always hated her, and now you have left me with her to go through all of your shit!" she shrieks. Directly in front of me, a woman rages against her husband, who committed suicide with no warning signs after decades of marriage. "Why did you leave me here alone, with this house I **can't sell**!" she howls, pounding with both hands and sobbing abjectly.

The air is charged and tingling in a way that reminds me of weather events. The energy being unleashed here feels capable of lifting cars, ripping up fence posts, upturning trees. I sit back on my haunches, slackened and vacated completely, as I listen to the squall. I close my eyes and think of watching lightning storms from my mother's lap on our front porch: I am witness to impressive, elemental violence, but I am safe and warm inside of it.

I look back at Stacy, whose eyes are shining and cheeks are pink; unbidden, we grin at each other.

✧

After the pillow pounding, we all stand around, mixing warmly with strangers. "Guys, I'd just like to say that I am touched by your bravery," a dark-haired woman in a cowled sweater and loose-fitting pants says, touching Stacy's elbow. She is here, we find out, mourning her husband, who isn't even dead: years ago, he had been bitten by a mosquito and contracted West Nile. It had destroyed his mind and turned him, as she says, "into a two-year-old with adult strength." He became dangerous, and she moved him to a full-time facility. Her mother-in-law accused her of abandoning him and hasn't spoken to her since. "It's time that I moved on from him," she says sadly. "The man I married died years ago."

Grief, I am learning, is a world you move

into—a world of softer voices, gentler gazes, closer observation, heightened compassion. It is, in many ways, a beautiful and redemptive place to spend time, and everyone at Kripalu has given themselves over completely to it by now. There is beauty here, all around us—in this woman's watchful compassion despite her own heavy life, and in the immediacy and warmth in which we find ourselves responding to her. If you allow it to be, grief can be a soothing stone temple where you hear only the murmured echoes of your own voice and the voices of your fellow travelers. None of us is expected to accomplish anything concrete while we are here, or to rise to any particular occasion. The mundanities have burned off, and only ultimate meaning remains.

Before we leave, Stacy works up the courage to approach Maureen. Over three sessions in two days, we have received no word from Greta. We had hoped Callie, Kevin and Melissa's daughter, might find Greta in the room and hold her hand; perhaps the two of them together could make themselves known to Maureen. But every time her eyes dilated, scanning the crowd, they alit and focused on someone else; another attendee got to have a message from the beyond. The weekend is over now, after a group photo, and people are starting to drift into the hall, to the doors. I feel Stacy yearning next to me, and I turn to her: "You should go," I urge. She stands up and wanders over to Maureen, who is chatting with someone by the podium up front.

Stacy returns a few minutes later, her eyes clouded and battling disappointment.

"Well?" I ask.

"She didn't get much," Stacy says sadly. "I told her our story, and she held my hand. She said she was just getting little flashes, no words."

I press her. "She didn't see anything? What kind of flashes? Did she get a picture of anything?"

"The one thing she said she saw clearly was a balloon. One balloon. I don't know, does that mean anything to you?"

I am electrified by this. "Stacy, oh my god," I say. "Don't you remember? The day on the rooftop."

The previous summer, Stacy and I had done

a yoga class on a roof deck every Thursday.
The teacher lived on the top floor of a six-
story building looking over Coney Island
Avenue, and her apartment, improbably, had
a wraparound deck. From the remove of the
deck, even Coney Island Avenue felt serene.
We would go every week, after work, gazing
up at the blue as music played softly from
her iPhone, plugged into a portable speaker.
Her six-year-old son, Justin, would occasionally break loose from whatever movie was
keeping him occupied to come outside and
run across all the mats, shouting. Sometimes
her dog would come outside and yap at us
in **savasana,** our eyes closed and our limbs
melting. But the happy mess of her life felt
integrated seamlessly into everything, and
after class we would eat fresh fruit and watch
the setting sun burn the rooftops on the
skyline.

One such class, we were on our backs,
twisting to one side and gazing up, when I
spotted a purple balloon, a single dot, sailing
clear across the cloudless blue sky. I pointed
to it and quietly said to Stacy, for some reason
I couldn't fathom, "That's Greta," and Stacy

began sobbing unaccountably next to me. She felt the truth of it.

Sitting at Kripalu, I feel the chill pass through Stacy as it passes through me. Greta was obsessed with balloons—specifically, the way they flew away from you. It was one of the first lessons I taught her about lack of control. We were around the corner from our building, lingering on some interesting crack in the sidewalk or at one of the skinny trees, when a couple with a toddler pushed past, their stroller festooned with white balloons, catching Greta's eye. The mother, kindly, untied one and handed it to us, and I tried to tie it to Greta's wrist. She was having none of it; she was going to hold on to the string.

"Well, then you really gotta hold on tight, OK?" I told her, feeling the comical inevitability of what would happen next.

Sure enough, Greta took two steps before her grip loosened, and the balloon sailed up and nestled in the crook of a branch. Watching that slow-motion second of pre-meltdown pass over her stricken face, I stepped in to flood her with chatter.

"Look, Greta, the balloon flew up—up into the sky!" I pointed up at the balloon with great interest, as if the balloon's travels were the most interesting thing in the world, a natural phenomenon we might study together. "You had it in your hand, and then it went out of your hand, and now it's up there! Up there, in the tree! It flew away up into the sky!"

I kept repeating this, tracing the journey for her, treating the loss as matter-of-fact, one more thing we might chat about. Her face softened and grew pensive, her eyes deepening, and she said, tentatively, "It flew away? Up into the sky!"

Whenever anything was lost after that— her pacifier (which was hidden rather than lost, since she grew interested in it only when she pretended to be a baby), her milk bottle, a tiny stuffed doll, a toy car—that was how she processed it. "It flew away—up in the sky!" she would exclaim. The balloon was an object lesson about impermanence—the way of all things—that never left her.

"Pay attention to signs," Maureen had said in her final session with us, addressing the group. "You have to try to relax and accept them, be receptive. You have to turn off your skeptical mind, because that's something we all do—'Oh, well, of course I saw that penny on the street with the birth year of my father, it's just spare change'—even if you're not wrong, you're not going about it the right way. Seeing signs is about receptivity. You have to learn to be receptive. The spirits, they are always trying to reach us, but they can only do it with little signs like that. If you're not looking out for those signs, you're going to miss the opportunity to hear from them."

For the first time since Greta died, Stacy and I feel the curtain separating us from her spirit parting.

We drive home in awe. We see the skyline of the city approaching us, and we feel as if we are reentering it from another dimension. We pledge to keep this spirit alive in us, even as the city seeks to deafen it.

Four

SEARCHING FOR HOME

RETURNING FROM KRIPALU, WE ARE FACED finally with the rootlessness of our lives. It is nearly Thanksgiving, and for the past six months we have lived for nothing. The absence of meaning has been comforting in a way. We must like the feeling, because we keep doubling down on it: having lost Greta, it seems, we are experimenting with how much of ourselves we can harrow away and still technically exist.

First to go was our home. Greta was everywhere in it, padding agreeably around every corner. Being in our apartment where she was not, walking past the closed door of her empty bedroom and averting our eyes to use the bathroom, was unendurable. The grief books all said not to make any radical changes for at least a year after catastrophic loss. We quickly decided this was bullshit.

By July, Stacy had taken the lead, sorting real estate listings according to price, to neighborhood, to number of bedrooms, to condominium vs. co-op. In moments of great transition in our lives, I tended to become cargo: Stacy would plot the course, and if I had the presence of mind, I scrambled for the rudder. There was something spiritual in her ability to map the contours of our future, to trace its corners and wrestle with its logistics, before it came into view. **There has to be something up ahead in this blackness, so let's start taking measurements.**

Her real estate search occupied most of her free hours, and the rest of her time was spent getting rid of paint cans, old sweaters, electronics. The clutter that I had pushed to the top shelves of our closets on her orders suddenly began whispering to her, and I found myself on a ladder, dragging it all back down to the carpet. We dropped bags of our old clothes at recycling; we got rid of stray connectors and RCA cords. At night, we sat on the couch as Stacy scrolled through listings. We liked this floor plan; we didn't like how old that building was; there **had** to be a reason that one was that cheap; oh my god, the maintenance on this building was insane. "I only want to throw things away and look at real estate," Stacy declared to me.

There was something else alive in the air between us—something we'd been too afraid to prematurely identify as "hope," but we recognized the weather conditions for it. One night, while discussing the move, Stacy said it: "We can't do it all over again here."

I had already discovered this thought living in my heart: I wanted to be a father again. But I did not simply want to be "a father" again. I wanted to be **Greta's** father. I liked Greta's father. Greta's father was bursting with pride and happiness, even when he was exhausted and frazzled. Sometimes I still expected to look up and see Greta and me laughing and walking together down the block, as if observing my old self from a great distance.

✧

Just as we began our apartment search, a report was published in **The New York Times.** How is it that a chunk of windowsill simply fell eight stories to strike a child? Although no one thought to notify the parents, the city apparently commissioned an inquiry on Greta's behalf, and the Department of Investigation was dispatched to find out the answer.

According to the city's report, the senior center around the corner from Grandma Suz's, where she and Greta regularly stopped and chatted with the residents, was certified "OK-SAFE" by an inspector who never visited the building. He never saw it, never even stood across the street with binoculars. He did not observe the large, S-shaped crack in the facade that telegraphed such imminent danger that an inspector across the street, working on a completely different building, sent an email about it to the Department of Buildings. Someone responded to that, the **Times** reported, but no action was taken.

There were hundreds of other buildings across New York City that had safety-code violations just as severe, it turned out.

After the report, the falling brick began its gruesome replay in my mind again—forever spiraling out into free space, crushing the firing brain of my Greta. I started thinking a lot about the word "mortified." "I was so mortified," people will say—**I was so embarrassed, I was made to feel like nothing but a body.** "I died," people also say, but that doesn't pack the same oomph: all college English students eventually read John Donne's "The Canonization" only to have the professor, eyes twinkling, explain what "we die and rise the same" really meant. To die was romantic, even sexual. "Mortified" had that stiffening current coursing through it, the threat of lowering temperatures.

Greta didn't die. Greta was **mortified**. The brick was a grievous insult sent from the universe, a refutation of her small hopes, dreams, plans. Now, her spirit was diffused, a comet trail of dashed expectations.

In the wake of the report, the city I'd called home for ten years was suddenly too loud, too noisy, too dangerous. I looked up wherever I walked, thinking something could fall at any time. I crossed the street to avoid scaffolding and sidewalk sheds, a completely irrational response since a lack of both killed Greta. As I darted under air-conditioning units that groaned out of windows, like overripe fruit ready to drop, I wondered: Was I simply rooted to the spot of my trauma, unable to muster the bravery to imagine leaving? Should we leave the city forever?

"After 9/11, I saw two kinds of patients," said my therapist. "People who considered leaving and people who left. None of them were wrong. This may change, but I've been talking to you now for a few months, and you sound to me like the people who don't leave."

She was right, we thought. We couldn't imagine it, even now. We had spent too long, poured too much of ourselves into this inhospitable climate, and now we were like two trees growing straight out of the side of a cliff; having adapted to life here, we felt unsuited to flourish anywhere else.

So as the trees began to yellow, we drove to an open house in Crown Heights. It was a gorgeous day, families everywhere—children sitting on fathers' shoulders and toddlers Greta's age on scooters. The apartment was a three-bedroom, with elementary-school children's drawings framed on the walls. The boy's bedroom, eerily well organized for a showing, was painted bright red, with sports pennants and posters and trophies. We wandered through the empty home, feeling like ghosts.

"It's beautiful," we told the woman standing around collecting names and trying not to loom. We left as quickly as possible.

Next, we fell unaccountably in love with a duplex, an odd and charming cottage-like house on the fringe of Park Slope with a basement floor and a backyard. The layout was nonsensical—a little dollhouse veranda, barely big enough to stand on, opening onto a small yard only accessible by a shared hallway. But the patch of green, the promise of seclusion—these visions clouded our eyes. We made an offer, then were dismayed when it was accepted.

Suddenly Stacy was staying up half the night to pore over the floor plan, imagining where our two couches would fit, where we would park a stroller, how we would block off the stairs. "OK, I think I've got it," she announced every morning when I woke up, bringing me over to examine her latest floor plan. "Oh no, but then the changing table will block the window," she would realize, crestfallen.

"What if our media cabinet went over here?" I inquired, pointing to another corner.

We both considered that. "That could work," she conceded.

We went back to see the place to reassure ourselves, and I found myself slapping away mosquitoes—five, seven, nine—from the disconcertingly buggy backyard as the real estate agent sought to comfort us: "This is a really special place, and you guys had a real connection with it," she reminded us. We walked outside; it was a gorgeous, quiet block. Green-Wood Cemetery, an acres-long resting place that housed Leonard Bernstein and Jean-Michel Basquiat, lay just across the street. We mentioned, again, how morbid others might find that. We agreed, again, how oddly comforting it was.

Driving home, Stacy noticed a power sub-station at the end of the block. "Is that safe?"

"Of course," I answered reflexively, and then felt the discomfort sit in my stomach.

We googled it that night. From a UK

government website: "Studies show a link between living near or under high-voltage power lines can increase risk of childhood leukemia."

Reading it, I felt a little helpless, like someone who suddenly believed in chemtrails. Was it true? Maybe. It was probably true enough. What if it wasn't true at all? Even then, the insinuation, having hatched in our brains—**is it true?**—would haunt every moment.

Suddenly, the apartment was too small, too impractical, too far from the subway. We withdrew our bid. The knot in my stomach released, and Stacy began sleeping again. Apartment hunting while in shock, we were learning, was tricky business.

✧

Our apartment search went on and on, far beyond when our actual apartment sold in October, and we had to move out. The couple who bought our place seemed unpleasant, and Stacy and I felt a slight pang: these people would be sleeping in Greta's old room, the only room she ever knew. But without her crib or her toys or her pattering feet, it was just a room.

Movers came and relocated our couches, tables, and dressers to a storage pod. We packed about a month's worth of clothing and toiletries into a suitcase and distributed the remainder of our belongings across Brooklyn—Greta's car seat and all of our pictures in one couple's basement, our instruments in another. In the back of our car, we kept Greta's ashes, zipped in a red bag given to us by the funeral home. They sat on top of a bin filled with dry goods from our pantry: granola, tea bags, half-eaten bars of chocolate.

Half an hour later, I stood outside of my old building, where I already did not live. This was Greta's home, the front stoop where I watched her play with her neighbors. Watching her run and squeal with the other kids, I had imagined them growing older, sneaking out to visit one another in the basement, having sleepovers in one another's apartments. Now she and we were gone.

✧

After abandoning our home, we forswore family. The decision felt instinctual, more animal than conscious. We lacked the capacity to discern our motives. Maybe we were curling up like injured dogs? Scattering, roachlike, from scrutiny? We didn't know, and, more important, we didn't care. Not caring was a novel sensation to us, and we embraced it.

The break was less literal than our move—I spoke with my mother on the phone regularly, dully reporting on the facts of our dwindling existence—but I didn't hear a word of her bright voice in my ears, and when I hung up it was as if my parents had ceased to exist. Stacy and Susan, meanwhile, were an open wound. I avoided mentioning her at all to Stacy, only texting Susan privately once in a while. "We're on inner tubes, floating down a lazy river of grief," Susan told me. "We're on the same journey, but we don't control any of it."

We all saw one another exactly once. Hundreds of my coworkers and colleagues raised the money for a tree to be planted in Prospect Park in Greta's honor. My mother and father returned to Brooklyn for the planting on October 15, and Susan joined us.

Fall had been unusually dismal, and on the day of the planting, the cold was settling in, wind biting us from the duck pond. My parents looked grey and depleted in a way I'd never noticed before; Susan barely spoke apart from some mumbled pleasantries. She still seemed to be stranded in some purgatory, not really here. None of us was ready to be together, I realized.

After flipping through a pamphlet provided to us by the park, Stacy and I had settled on a black gum tree. In time, we'd read, it would sprout flaming-red teardrop leaves and grow tiny sour berries, which small birds would eat. We liked that idea.

The sapling looked weak and bare. Park volunteers labored quickly, lifting its squat base into a hole. We put a small laminated photo on the flimsy protective fence and then stood back to take stock of the effect. The planters left us in respectful silence.

I sat down next to Susan on a bench while she cried. She kept going until she had nothing left, and then she just stared out at the pond, emptied. My mother's hands gripped my shoulders, and I could feel her anger, her helplessness.

Just then, a beagle on a leash circled the base of the tree and lifted its leg. We shouted frantically to the dog walker, who looked at the photo, the fence, and then, as it slowly dawned, hurried off, horrified. We laughed about this later, a faint warmth finally touching us. Greta would have found it hilarious.

✧

After moving out, we embarked on a strange, itinerant crawl through Brooklyn that mirrored the directionlessness of our internal lives. We crashed on couches, we stayed in spare bedrooms. It was oddly like being in college again: we were forever on break, the bedraggled cause célèbre of adults who had things we did not—kitchens, clean sheets, children.

We played our roles as well as we could: babysitters, doers of dishes, dinner companions. We visited often with parents whose children were Greta's friends; I'd stoop down to the floor and play with the children as the adults drank and talked. I played with their toys and read them books and took goofy self-ies with them, and I did not cry later at night, even as I couldn't help but notice the ways in which they changed, physically and emotion-ally, in ways Greta never would. Their voices cleared up, their hair grew longer.

Greta never grew much hair; she was "our little baldy," as we fondly called her. "Oh, Stacy and Jack were bald forever," Susan would laugh, as Greta ran around her living room. "You didn't grow any hair until you were almost three years old, Stace!"

My mother confirmed the same about me. "When you were two and a half, you finally grew these long blond curls," she remem-bered. "Oh, I loved those curls. They were so beautiful."

The longest hairs on Greta's head were just above her ears. They were translucent and cobwebby, and they caught the light in a way that suggested dust motes floating in a win-dow. Once, gazing at herself in her toy mirror just above her toy kitchen, she brought up a hand to a wisp, touched it, and exclaimed, "My hair's getting so long!" We laughed about it for days.

Stacy and I used to joke that we could not begin to imagine Greta as an older person. "I can only imagine her hairless baby head on a slightly taller body," I'd say. I thought about how macabre this seemed now.

One day we found ourselves picnicking at Brooklyn Bridge Park with our former neighbor Amy and her son, Jacob, another friend of Greta's. Amy and Saul, her husband, were letting us sleep in their third-floor bedroom, and we were doing our best not to be in the way.

I spent the afternoon with Jacob, playing daddy. He ran up ahead of me, laughing. I chased him, tickled him, joked with him. I could feel from his eyes and the intensity of his attention that he loved me in his generous little-boy way. His chatter was a constant stream of need and curiosity, and he kept asking me to sit next to him. I held his hand while he balanced and walked on the upraised curb; I lifted him up and lowered him playfully into the tall weeds behind it. I chased him, and let him chase me, around an empty bicycle rack.

As we played, my parental sensors switched on. I knelt down in front of him and spoke quietly, drawing his attention to small things. Look at this small flower in the sidewalk crack. Where is your mommy? There she is, sitting over there with some food. Should we go over there and sit next to her? Yeah, I think so, too.

Jacob's smile illuminated some broken sanctum in me that hadn't seen or felt much light since the pain. Children didn't smile at you; they smiled **into** you, and I could feel my love for Greta seeking a transference point. I needed to care for and love a little person; my need was as profound as walking, now that I'd developed it. What child might I love now?

Stacy sat with Amy in a pocket of shade. I joined her with Jacob, who sat between his mother and me. I looked at him, thinking how far away we were from nurturing a life like his. I wondered if my Greta, who once kissed Jacob on a playground in the cold of winter—their cheeks red from the wind and Jacob grinning like a man who'd won the lottery afterward—was watching us.

On the drive home, I sat next to Jacob in his car seat, keeping him occupied and awake so that his nap didn't begin in the car. He was giddy, approaching exhaustion and meltdown, and his laughter had a dangerous edge. We pulled up to Saul and Amy's house, and suddenly Jacob asked me, "Jayson, do you have a baby in your house?"

I felt Amy stiffen in the front seat. No one said a word. Greta had completely disappeared into the murky depths of his toddler's psychology. It was unclear to me if Jacob was aware of her ever having existed.

"No, Jacob," I managed. "No, we don't."

Jacob persisted: "But **why** don't you have a baby in the house?"

"I don't know, Jacob, little guy," I said, my voice breaking a little. "We just don't." I was unable to offer him anything else, because this was the truest answer. We just didn't.

I helped him out of his car seat and carried him up to their front door; he was already limp and pliable. I closed my eyes and smelled his hair. His little head rested on my shoulder and some part of me flickered alive, if only for a moment.

✧

We left Saul and Amy's house. They protested we could stay indefinitely, but being underfoot in another family's routine had only heightened our sense of rootlessness. So we checked into a three-hundred-square-foot studio on Airbnb; our renter, a bachelor named Asaf, left us a twelve-dollar bottle of Merlot as a welcoming gift. A visible inch of dust covered everything when we walked in. We set down our bags and got to work: Stacy scrubbed the toilet bowl while I passed a roll of paper towels over every surface, each one turning up black.

It was in these highly unromantic surroundings that we decided to begin trying again. We'd had unprotected sex a number of times since the summer, but after a week in "Asaf's Kingdom" (the wry name we gave the place, based on its Wi-Fi name), we bought several boxes of fertility tests. After a few nights, the applicator screen smiled at us, and we acted accordingly. There was comfort in the act, in the closeness and intimacy, but no hope—not yet. We were performing the act of hope, watering irradiated soil.

Stacy lay on her back on the bed, her legs up the wall. I lay next to her, with my legs jokingly up the wall, too. Our faces were a few inches apart: Her cheeks were slightly pink, a strand of hair falling over her slim, aquiline nose with its slight bump in the middle. Her eyes went deep and still in the moments right after. "Isn't it crazy that we find ourselves doing this again?" Stacy wondered, her gaze searching mine.

After, as when we were conceiving Greta, there was something luminous and mysterious in her eyes, a recession into some deep, private corridor—the wordless place, where all her deepest emotions roiled. I could see her as a small child in these moments, smaller and more frightened but lit from within by the same powerful emotional intelligence, the kind that allowed her to see other people's motivations more clearly than they saw their own. I imagined how lonely and bewildering it might have been growing up with this intuition. Greta had my round, moonlike face, my smile that turned slightly crooked and goofy in the lower left corner—but she had Stacy's eyes, crystal blue and fathomless.

I turned my head to take in our surroundings: "At least our accommodations are nicer," I joked. "Remember when we started dating? The first time you came over to my apartment, with that twin bed?"

"Oh my god, your towel smelled **so bad**." Stacy laughed. "I **still** remember how gross your shower was. Oh god."

"It's like we've gone backward in time," I said softly. I glanced down at her freckled and pale right shoulder, at her new tattoo: a delicate sparrow, beak parted and open, as if singing.

We had agreed in the wake of the accident that we would each get tattoos commemorating her, but Stacy sprang into action while I vaguely entertained the idea. A sparrow, she decided.

She spent the summer researching and perusing artist portfolios for hours, settling on a woman named Sajra, on the Lower East

Side. Her work was largely black and white and full of symbols: third-eye chakras, half-moons, coyote heads. She did exquisite birds. The day of her tattoo appointment, Stacy—who had successfully returned couches two months after purchasing them, mattresses for being an eighth of an inch too saggy, shoes for having a "weird" strap—woke up in the morning, smiled at me, said, "I'll see you in a few hours," and left serenely for a permanent body alteration.

I went to meet her a few hours later, when the tattoo was nearly finished. Sajra was still detailing. I held Stacy's hand and watched her face as the needle dug: "It feels more annoying than painful," she reported.

The three of us were the only ones there. The lights were off, and late-morning sunlight flooded the parlor. There was soft, gentle music playing—Hope Sandoval's voice, deep and dark and still. Sajra, who also did body work, handed Stacy a few healing crystals to hold on to during the inking. "Keep them," she said at the end.

The healing process began the next day, and with it came the delayed panic. "It's supposed to get all scabby like that, right?" Stacy asked me in the morning, poking at it hesitantly. The bird's delicate pinhole eye, made with white ink, had swollen into an ominous mole; the wings had grown craggy. "He looks more like a raven than a sparrow now."

Following instructions she pulled up on her phone for tattoo care, she washed it and dabbed it as lightly as she could with a paper towel. The paper towel stuck, and she pulled first gingerly, then in a panic. "It's **sticking**!" Her eyes popped as she held the towel out in front of me. "Look," she cried. "The whole tattoo is on there!"

I looked at the towel, which had the faint imprint of the bird, like a bas-relief, on its Bounty squares. "If it were that easy to ruin a tattoo, Stacy, everyone's tattoo would be ruined," I said, for probably the tenth time that afternoon. This would pass, I told myself.

For the next several days, Stacy fretted obsessively about the bird and its puffed-up eye. "Goddamn it," she said. "I never should have put that towel on it. I should have just left it alone."

The days mounted, as did Stacy's apologetic follow-up emails to Sajra. As her mania continued, friends fondly rolled their eyes at me in solidarity—**Stacy and her obsessions.** But the sparrow's eye was a portal, I knew. You could never begin to answer the questions swarming around us—what did it mean to honor Greta? how could we carry forth her spirit?—but you could thread them through a tattooed sparrow's eye. That was a problem you could pick at, literally and metaphorically.

As her skin slowly settled, so did she. In ten days, the bird grew more delicate and less haggard looking, and its delicate white pupil reemerged from the melanoma-like eye bump. Stacy pulled up her shirt sleeve proudly about two weeks later at dinner. "I have regrets about everything, and I don't have any regrets about this," she joked.

The sparrow had multiple meanings. "They're city birds," Stacy told me. "They kind of make do with what they have, like us." Sparrows, besides pigeons, were the only birds Greta ever saw. "Lookit the birdies," Greta would call to me, pointing as they hopped across the sidewalk and fluttered up into the tiny saplings lining the broken-up sidewalk to her daycare.

It also came from the last book we bought and read to Greta, called **The Lion and the Bird**. In it, a gentle lion farmer scoops up a wounded bird that falls into his field. He mends its wing and brings it to his house, where he keeps it warm through the winter. Several pictures show them braving the cold, the bird nestled in his mane; the two of them enjoying a crackling fire together; and the two of them asleep, the bird lying in the lion's sandal, next to his bed. It is a book about the inevitable: the bird's wing heals, the thaw passes, and the bird flies away. "Yes, I know," the lion says to the bird; it is the only line of dialogue in the book. The next page, a double-page spread of white with just the lion gazing skyward, always left me in tears.

The next few pages show the lion, crest-fallen, going about his life. The same fields, the same fire, the same bed—no bird. "Sometimes life is like that," the book advises. The winds blow colder, and the lion catches himself looking up: "Well?" he wonders. There are a few pages of agonizing delay, a false

start, a falling leaf. And then the bird swoops
down, lands on a branch, regards the lion.
They will tough out another winter in each
other's company.

After Greta's death, the book became intolerable to me; we were living the life of that
lion, with no promise of the bird's return.
Every day, we got up, made breakfast, show-
ered, dressed, and walked into the world,
without our sparrow.

In bed at Asaf's Kingdom, I reached down
and traced the lines of its beak tenderly. The
bird was fragile and full of light, as if I could
reach out and cup its warmth in my palm.
One claw was visible, perched atop a crescent
moon. The open beak was inclined to Stacy's
right ear. "Is she singing to you?" I asked Stacy.
A few tears sprang to the almond corners of
her eyes and leaked down onto the bedspread.

"Yeah, sometimes she is," she whispered.

✦

Finally, we walked into an open house and
knew: this was the place. It was a second-story
brick condo near the water, and we loved it

the second we entered. We brushed past the other nervous open-house attendees, trying to fight the instinctive panic of possessiveness— **It's ours! We deserve it more than all of you!**—that rose up in us. We squeezed past a midthirties woman who had brought her mother and stood alone in the second bedroom. Bunk beds. The family had raised two children, a boy and a girl, to middle school in this second-floor Brooklyn apartment, one of the agents informed us. Stacy and I, awaiting the results of our latest ovulation-test experiment, glanced at each other meaningfully.

Driving back from the viewing, we jabbered endlessly to each other. "I could really see us there for ten years, at least," Stacy kept saying. "It's a good school district, and there are gardens everywhere! It feels like life would actually be easier there. Don't you think?"

I did. But I was unable to do much except nod. As always, Stacy's indomitable sense of forward motion continued to tug us into the future even when I was listless and drifting. I stole a look at her eyes as she drove; they were blazing and clear. We would have to find a sublet, she reasoned. If they accepted our offer, maybe we could try to close by mid-December? I strained to keep up. She dictated an email to our realtor as she turned onto the Brooklyn-Queens Expressway, which I dutifully tapped into her phone, holding up a hand occasionally to plead **wait, wait**.

We submitted our offer the following day; that night, we made love again on Asaf's scratchy IKEA comforter. The excitement we felt was both invigorating and awful, like breathing freezing air. My nerves were shattered, and yet optimism coursed through them anyway. I was hardwired, I realized. If you were built for optimism, you just had to figure out a way to stay that way. We couldn't keep not caring, even if we wanted to; we just weren't made for it. I felt an unexpected throb of empathy for pessimists: **You can't help it, either.**

✧

It is December. Our bid has been accepted, but the closing date has once again been pushed back. Now, we are sitting in the last

Airbnb of our long, enervating period of homelessness. We have been living out of the same bag for two months. There is no Wi-Fi in this apartment. There is an AT&T card you buy from a corner bodega and refill. There is one knife in the kitchen, and it is barely fit for carving pumpkins. Nonetheless, we have been cooking almost every night, having nearly snapped from night after night of takeout and restaurants.

Tonight we are eating dried-out beans and underdone rice out of tiny chipped plastic bowls. We are drinking bad wine out of coffee mugs.

Frustrated, depressed, I decide to go out to buy some chocolate for dessert. I end up pacing the street. It is horribly cold, everything is closed, and I lose it; somehow the lack of chocolate breaks me, overwhelming me with desolation. Stacy keeps texting me: "Are you almost home? Come back." I text her a string of expletives. She texts, "I have something that will make you feel better." In my black cloud, I feel certain I know what she is talking about. She is about to show me the latest sketch of the built-in shelving unit she is planning. I have been looking at various iterations of this sketch for days and have run out of helpful-sounding noises to make.

When I walk in the door, sour and despondent, Stacy tells me gently to close my eyes. I look at her. "OK," I say. I close my eyes. I wait, impatiently. I hear her feet creak across the floorboards as she makes her way back toward me.

"Open your eyes," she says softly.

I open my eyes.

I am looking at a white plastic stick with a tiny screen.

It says PREGNANT.

Five

PREGNANCY

SINCE GRETA'S ACCIDENT, Stacy's mother, Susan, has grown increasingly reclusive. She won't answer texts for ten, fourteen days at a stretch, and when she finally does we discover she hasn't left her apartment and has spent the entire time in bed. She's aged thirty years, it seems: her hands tremble from psych meds for her PTSD, and she's lost the ability to focus on tasks for more than an hour, which means she is hemorrhaging work.

She emerges from her exile to visit us after Christmas. Through a sort of tacit agreement, we'd all skipped Christmas Day, and aside from the tree planting, this is the first time we've all been in the same room in months. Stacy and I had finally moved into our new place, and after a few weeks getting it in working order—built-in bookshelf installed in the living room, rugs put down, floors and surfaces scrubbed clean—it was time to bring family into it.

Also, there was the minor matter of breaking our news.

The mood is festive, but tentative and fragile: being in the same room sometimes feels like visiting a blast site, and we are all a little wary in one another's company. Stacy and I confer silently at the counter while I open another bottle of champagne. **Now? No, not now.**

Jack and Stacy rib Susan good-naturedly about her unconventional mothering techniques. "Remember in high school, when I slept over at Amanda's house and got drunk without telling you? You called her house and left the world's most insane voice message." Stacy launches into an impersonation: **"Somebody! Needs to! Reel you! The fuck! In!"** Susan doubles over.

"I used to bring my friends over just to show them that you let us swear in front of you," Jack says from the fridge, opening his third beer. "Nobody believed me. So I'd bring them over and just start yelling, 'Fuck! Fucking shit, Mom!'"

Susan is helpless now, wiping tears from the corners of her eyes. "The research has vindicated me on that," she cries. "It clearly shows that children who are allowed to swear grow up to be more intelligent."

"You see, Mom?" Stacy prods. "If you lived in Brooklyn, it could always be like this."

"I **love** my building," Susan replies, her smile stiffening slightly and the room hardening with it.

No one quite understands Susan's insistence on remaining on the Upper West Side, around the corner from the bench where her granddaughter was killed. But she clings to her apartment like a life raft in a roaring ocean, tortured by continuous flashbacks but seemingly unable to contemplate upending her life once again. Inside, she feels safe enough: there is a plaque and a tree dedicated to Greta in the little garden, and the doormen check on her daily. But the moment she steps outside, the world swarms and she panics. One day, a car backfired and she collapsed, hysterical, on the sidewalk.

Lesley tries to shift the mood. "Does

anyone need more champagne? Stacy?" She leans forward to fill Stacy's glass before she can object. I move in to smoothly intercept the glass, but everyone notices, and I catch Susan and Jack exchanging meaningful looks. So it probably isn't a surprise by the time I turn the music down, Stacy and I sit in opposite chairs facing them all on the couch, and Stacy says, "So, we have some news."

Susan reacts with joy and terror: "Oh my god, I'm so excited and happy for you," she says, welling up. Then, her voice still watery, she adds as an afterthought, "I should probably move to Scotland."

We all laugh: **What?!** But nothing seems unreasonable in these circumstances, and the tangible prospect of hope, the looming threat and promise of new life, is a crazy-making thing. The ground is heaving once more beneath us, and we behave like skittish animals sensing a storm. We hug one another, teary and smiling, and then everyone abruptly leaves. We need to be alone again.

✧

I am waiting for Stacy to meet me outside a yoga studio when I spot her walking up the block. She's at that early stage of pregnancy, not yet showing but emitting some mysterious pheromonal signal, so an unusually attuned few start to look at her differently. You can almost see the thought bubble over their heads as they walk past: **Is she . . . ? Are they . . . ?**

As she gets closer, her face comes into focus. She is flustered and upset, walking too fast and with her hands balled at her sides. "I just had an awful conversation with my mom," she tells me. "She just told me that she's not **ever** going to move. I got emotional and had to hang up."

Since we announced the pregnancy, Susan and Stacy have been fighting continuously. The incidentals change, but the underlying tension does not: Susan feels forever misunderstood, while Stacy feels she understands all too well. It is an echo of the fight they've had their whole lives, but it's taken on uglier dimensions in Greta's absence. Greta was the fragile bridge Stacy and Susan walked across;

now they stand on opposite sides of a gulf, each unable to hear the other.

"Oh no. Did you ask her why? What did she say?"

"She says it's where all her **memories** are," Stacy says, drawing out "memories" venomously. "Forget that her entire family is in Brooklyn and that we're never going to the Upper West Side again. She knows that." Stacy stops, takes in a shaky breath. "I just . . . I wish she didn't make decisions like this."

As usual with Stacy's family, the right words elude me. "I hope she changes her mind" is all I say. We enter the studio and set up.

Twelve weeks into Stacy's second pregnancy, we are still doing yoga together three, sometimes four times a week. It probably resembles discipline to onlookers, this compulsion, but there is a desperation lurking in our devotion that makes me flinch when I stop to notice it. We live in constant terror of reverting to our childless days before Greta, when we slumped around purposelessly for entire weekends—we would have failed her, and oblivion would have claimed her. So we commit furiously to our yoga schedule.

We've found ourselves drawn to the fastidiousness of Iyengar yoga, which makes a point, nearly a fetish, of alignment. The simple poses you do in other classes become quantum physics problems, and standing is no longer a single act but dozens of them—heels spreading into the floor, thighs and knees lifting. I am grateful for this complicated instruction partly for how it disperses the weight of my existence into little shreds; life feels more manageable when I am directing all of my attention and energy toward my left big toe bone.

Other classmates filter in, wave silently to us as we settle in.

"Allow your eyes to soften and unfocus, letting the light in but not holding it," says our teacher Mimi. "Allow your upper lids to draw over the eyeball, until your eyelids meet."

I try to embrace this peculiar instruction, to discover something new and strange in an eye blink. I can feel Stacy settling in next to me, her breathing starting to even. I close my eyes, and when my lids finally meet, I find Greta, like a finger pad touching the surface of an old, cool scar. I smile in recognition. **Hi, sweetie,** I whisper silently.

I stretch both arms high up above my head and feel my internal organs lift, releasing a flood of memories and sensation like dishes clattering to the floor. I lean into my forward leg, my arms supplicating skyward. Greta's fluttering fingers after she nursed at two weeks old come to me, her head tilted and her eyes closed as if she were conducting an underwater symphony. "She's milk drunk," Stacy would say tenderly. I am rewarded by tears releasing down my face, warm and silent as sweat. Mimi and Stacy and the rest of the class disregard me. This part, too, is routine.

We fold at our waists over stiffened legs.

"**Look** at your knees," Mimi commands. "Can you see them lift? **Lift** them, and then don't lift them. Do you see the difference?"

Mimi is obsessed with knees, constantly exhorting us to lift them, to observe them. I stare obediently, and as my fingertips graze my toes, Greta appears before me in her purple one-piece swimsuit. Her legs protrude like stubby frankfurters, her face beet red and her little hairs matted with sweat. "I don't wanna be outside annnnyyyymorre," I hear her say—she had recently learned the word "anymore," drawing it out, and she somehow knew exactly how to use it.

I straighten, bring my feet together, inhale. I remember how her hands felt exploring the contours of my face. **Tadasana,** standing pose. I am instructed to imagine my pelvis as a bowl full of water I cannot spill. I remember Greta's legs gripping my hip. I remember her sticky fingers in my hair, the look of focus on her face as she "fixed" it.

Most days, these memories streak by in a blur, and my inability to see them clearly feels alarmingly like forgetting. I can feel my mind doing it: I am abridging her, whittling down months of our daily existence into stand-in moments. The afternoon I tied a purple balloon to Greta's shirt and she drove herself mad with joy and frustration, grabbing and letting it go and watching it float inches above her face—that has become the cover photo for a mental file labeled "Greta, 12–14 months." My mind never opens the file, and I worry it is because it is empty.

I shot a sixteen-second video of this

moment, which took place after Danny and Elizabeth's daughter Clara's fourth birthday. Our pictures from the party itself are haphazard, which oddly means I remember it more vividly: my mind has to work overtime to fill in the gaps, to supply smells and sounds. Of the balloon, I can recall only the slight slipping I experienced whenever I snapped a perfect picture. Now that she's gone, I understand what this feeling meant: it was the sound of my brain off-loading a task. **We can let this one go.** The more you photograph, the more you permit yourself to forget.

I have thumbed through her existing photos and videos so many times, so hungrily, that my reactions to them have dimmed: they feel used up somehow. I remain haunted by the thought there is more of her, somewhere, yet to be rescued from the digital ether. Maybe, if I just kept looking, I would be delivered her flushed red cheeks again, the light lines beneath her eyes.

I am on my back with my legs angled up a wall. The lights are dimmed, and Mimi has placed weighted sacks on the soles of my feet. Stacy lies next to me, and I can tell from the flickering on her face that she feels sick again. Class is just about over, and we will need to hurry to get her something to eat so her nausea will recede.

Stacy's sickness is easily twice as intense this time. Most days I come home from work to find her on her back, a hand on her forehead. She has a phobia of vomiting, so the bile stays clamped down while she moans. The nausea is a helpful distraction, in a way: there is something clarifying about her immediate misery, the way it robs us of our ability to think about the future or ponder its meaning.

We leave the studio as quickly as possible, Stacy fumbling for a Ziploc of her always-ready almonds and popping about twelve to fight back the queasiness. We settle across from each other at a café nearby, drinking scalding-hot coffees. I feel wrung out, cool, clear; it is this brief and quickly eroding peace that yoga provides as well. For a few minutes, my mind stops trying to solve the problem of Greta's not being here.

There is a buzz, and Stacy pulls her phone out, furrowing her brow. "It's my mom again," she says, typing back something forcefully.

She rolls her eyes, mutters, "Goddamn it," and slaps the phone facedown on the table.

"What did she say?"

"Oh, you know. Not an apology. An **explanation**."

"Should I . . . ?"

"I don't know," Stacy snaps, her eyes watering. We sit.

"I know I should be more sympathetic, but her helplessness makes me **so mad**," she says after a moment. "And she shoots me down when I try to help anyway. She's dismissive of everything I say."

When Stacy is upset, she pulls in from all corners—her shoulders bunch and knot, her lips press together, and her eyes go distant, as if shells have clicked over them. Watching her, I think of self-protecting organisms pulling themselves inside an exoskeleton, a gesture toward invincibility when they are at their most helpless.

Susan texts me irritably: "I'm sorry, but it will be a long time before I will be able to talk to Stacy again. She misinterprets everything I say. She accuses me of trying to make everything about me. She hangs up on me

90 percent of the time, saying, 'I can't talk about this with you.' I can't do it. I can't be her punching bag anymore."

"We are all the walking wounded," I remind her. "We are all hurting, and we hurt each other. I love you."

That night, Stacy cries hard in my arms. I hold her, staring at the ceiling, thinking that no matter the evidence mustered on either side, the case made, there is one thing that an arguing parent and child will always both be right about: **You didn't know what it felt like to be me.**

✧

We go for our first sonogram. We choose a new clinic, across the city from where Greta was born. No one there knows about us—not the woman who asks us to sign in without looking up, or the technician who retrieves us from the waiting room where CNN is blaring.

"OK, if mama could get up on the table and pull up your shirt, we can get started," she says, and I watch it all happen again in front of me: the cold gel smeared from the squelching tube, the large, awkward Doppler. I watch the black of the screen as the rubber head touches down on Stacy.

There is a moment or two of confusion, a growling sound as the tip searches blindly. "Hold a second," the technician murmurs, more to herself than to us, turning delicate circles with her wrist and keeping her eyes on the monitor. The room is filled with buffeting noise and the screen with white. We wait, breath held, for the confusion to resolve itself.

Then, suddenly, clarity breaks, and an urgent thumping noise fills the tiny room. "There we go," she says, a note of professional satisfaction in her voice. I had forgotten the startling velocity of a fetus's heartbeat, like a drowning man's breaths as he breaks through the surface. **WOMWOMWOM-WOMWOMWOMWOM.**

The sound fills the tiny room; it is loud and urgent and all out of proportion to the wisp of tissue fluttering in water on-screen. Stacy's right hand grabs mine, squeezing so hard my fingertips go cold. As I watch the fragile clump of cells busily subdividing, I feel a curious sensation coursing through my veins. It is unnamable: there is dread, but joy, too. The first round of antibiotics entering an infected patient, perhaps, or a prompt urging a wrecked system back online.

"Congratulations, guys," says the technician. "Everything looks perfect."

We get on the elevator, a little speechless, clutching the little printout with the date and our nameless second child floating on it. As we take the elevator down, I look at it, holding the very edges to keep from getting fingerprints on it. At the center of this little translucent cloud of mingling DNA, a storm is brewing, a million detonations happening soundlessly every second. The being at the center of it is forming already, choosing its road to creation one forked genetic path at a time. Even as the elevator dings on the bottom floor and opens onto the lobby, even as we walk, stricken, into the street, that life is coming further into focus.

The next day on the train to work, I begin, tentatively, to talk to my unborn child, making small promises to him or her. "Hi there, little one," I venture. My tongue feels thick, like I am recovering after a stroke. "We heard your heartbeat yesterday. It was very strong! You sound like a determined little one. You are going to learn a lot very quickly. Light, dark—first you have to learn about that. You have to learn to feel safe when your hands aren't bundled. You have to learn how to drink milk from your mommy's breast. It's a lot to remember. You will do great, though; I am very excited for you to learn.

"I am going to have lots of work to do, too," I tell the child. "I am going to have to learn to make the world feel safe for you. This is Daddy's problem, not yours. He is going to make absolutely certain you understand the world is a safe, good place."

❖

My office has relocated to downtown Manhattan, to One World Trade Center. From my new window, I can gaze down directly into the pits of the original towers, now fountains engraved with the names of thousands dead. Down here at the tapered tail of the island, the buildings bunch together, stand shoulder to shoulder, leering at me. Every corner is livid and ablaze with construction, heavy objects erupting like gunshots on corrugated steel and jackhammers turning up chunks of the street beneath me.

If we are truly going to bring another child into this city, I tell myself, **the least I can do is to teach them not to live in fear.** As I think this, a father puts a child on a yellow bus, and I watch in consternation as it rattles off, nearly brushing the side view mirrors of every parked car in its way.

I pace and turn down another side street, feeling it build inside me. There is only one other person in sight, a jogger up the block. I slow down and wait until he passes just out of sight. I take a chance and I open my mouth and I scream—a short, sharp, bottled sound. I feel the rewarding rush of some endorphins; I hear my voice ricochet off the clustered buildings, formidable and full of pain. I listen to the echoes die and feel powerful for once. **You can't hurt us.**

After this, I become a prospector for safe screaming spaces in New York. There are eight million people in this city—what are the odds I might find a corner of it to howl like a man being stabbed without being heard by a single one of them? My success rate surprises me. Early-morning malls, before the shops have raised their shutters; one-way streets deep in Brooklyn's industrial sector, surrounded by nothing but parked trucks and vacant warehouses: these are ripe spaces for my experiments, and I make the city quake, rattling loose screws and hearing myself bounce off walls.

Once or twice, I miscalculate. Underground, I utter three sharp, gasping shouts, like someone whose hand has been crushed by a train. A man runs out suddenly from a corner newsstand, eyes wild: he sees me, alone.

I have nothing to tell him; I simply wave him away.

✧

Now that our public grief rituals have faded from view, we've been forced to come up with private ones like these. And like all life born in the cracks, our private grief rituals

are **weird:** warped and inexplicable. I think
of the Greenland shark, a four-hundred-year-
old creature that made the news recently due
to its gruesomeness: its sticky, putrid flesh is
poisonous to the touch, an adaptation to life
miles from sunlight. I can feel similar things
living in my gut, unrecognizable to me and
surely adapting to live just as long.

I have started to carry around little gift-
shop Zen books like Pema Chödrön's **When
Things Fall Apart.** I say "carry around"
because I don't even read it, really: I just
take it out of my bag on the subway and
hold it, running my thumb along the spine.
Occasionally I jot down little quotes from it,
nonsense like "Everything that occurs is not
only usable and workable but is actually the
path itself." When I read them the first time,
they glow hot with meaning, but the next day
I find them dull and cold again.

My mother tells me she has taken to
manically mulching the soil around the
pink hydrangeas she has planted in honor of
Greta—she is terrified they will not bloom
and talks to them continuously. "I need you
here, if you don't mind," she will whisper into

the mulch chips. "To celebrate your life and your beautiful spirit."

Stacy's brother, Jack, has been on a downward spiral since Greta's death. He stays out at bars every night, sometimes until six a.m. Ten, twelve, fourteen vodka sodas pass through his hands in a night, clearing the way for heavier, darker substances. He drinks beer in the shower the next day. He makes new friends or introduces us to old friends we've never met or heard of before. You can sense their discomfort and ambivalence at meeting us, feel the clamminess in their handshakes: these are the uneasy alliances forged deep in a committed nightlife, and they don't flourish in daylight. Jack is clear-eyed about all of this activity: this is his **Leaving Las Vegas**, it seems, a tribute performance for his late father.

As for Stacy, I am left to guess at the depths of her grief. As always, she prefers to hide in plain sight, deflecting attention and moving under cover of her inexhaustible sociability. Her relationship to Greta is a sealed sanctum, and I fight with a shameful hunger for glimpses into it.

As eloquent as she is with the emotions of others, she has always been deaf and mute to her own. When Stacy is upset or depressed, she will start to say something, trail off, and gesture irritably at me to fill in the blank. I am her interpreter; it is part of our deal.

It is easier for me, because I have all these words. They just fall out of me—they get everyone's attention, put form and shape and definition to my suffering. Stacy doesn't have words. Her grief for her lost daughter is a color, a cloud.

When I share with her how good it feels to scream, she admits, "I scream in the car sometimes. I have road rage anyway, so it's kind of a safe place." I have a brief flash of her doing this—her face contorted in startling wrath, pounding the steering wheel with the palm of her hand on the Prospect Expressway. The image is so vivid to me that I have a little shiver of empathy.

I'd seen Stacy grieve only once before, after the sudden death of her father, just six months after our wedding. At first we knew nothing—sudden, cause uncertain. Then a flurry of phone calls back and forth from

Charlottesville. An evasive call from her uncle, who refused to talk specifics. Then, in horrible slow motion, the details revealed themselves.

"There was a gun," Stacy told me simply, setting her phone back down in her lap a few hours later, after the truth had been pried loose. His body had been discovered by a friend, hours after he fired the shot, sitting on his bed.

I gaped at her and felt the floor give way beneath me. She no longer seemed to require my support. When her father was simply dead, no explanations, she had been inconsolable. But now that something far more horrible had revealed itself, she stopped crying and became eerily lucid and composed. She served as our guide through the next week, quietly making preparations and discussing logistics with her uncle. She navigated family dynamics. She shopped around for the right urn. She helped write the ceremony. I rarely saw her cry anymore. She was needed and, perhaps, was therefore relieved of the burden of needing anything.

Her father lived a truncated life according

to some basic convictions. He idolized tragic figures like Gram Parsons, Roky Erickson, Ian Curtis. He cut a rueful, wry, ruggedly handsome figure, a man of few words but probing intellect and discerning taste, and he bonded with Susan in college over narrow but intense shared interests: rock music, books, counterculture, food. He had a generous grin and a quiet manner; "You never knew what was behind that grin of his," a friend remembered fondly at his funeral.

As years went on, Susan began to want different things: New York City, art, music, new communities. Stacy's father wanted exactly the same thing, night after night, in Virginia: beers, steaks on the grill, the family gathered around the television. The divorce, when it finally happened, was long, ugly, and acrimonious. Stacy was in college; Jack was at home. At Stacy's graduation, her father lurked mournfully in the background, fearful of igniting a confrontation and ruining the event. He met Stacy in an alleyway afterward, handing her a card with a check while mumbling and crying silently. Then, still hoping to avoid creating a scene, he turned and skulked off into the night. Stacy still chokes up when she talks about it.

Her father moved to Charlottesville after the divorce, while his children followed their mother to set up in New York. Hundreds of miles from his family, he started acting the part of a divorcé—rented condo, Hawaiian shirts, new BMW with electrical issues. He had a massive television and a voluminous DVD library, heavy on exploitation and camp: **Rocky Horror, Motel Hell,** Roger Corman's **The Little Shop of Horrors, Pink Flamingos**.

When I met him, he had the ruddy face and broken capillaries of a man capable of drinking a handle of whiskey in a matter of hours. I watched him do just that our first night together without a noticeable change in his demeanor. There was something doleful in his figure, which slumped slightly, but an untouchable dignity of bearing in there, too, and I saw in his arched eyebrows and undimmed eyes an observer's mind still at work.

The night of his suicide, Stacy and I went

to dinner. We were still young, married only six months. I raised a glass to hers: "To the worst night of our lives," I said somberly.

Jack drove down to Charlottesville immediately and spent two weeks alone cleaning out his dead father's condo, taking loads out to the dumpster and selling off boxes of new shirts, ties still in their plastic wrapping. When Stacy and I joined him, the condo was nearly empty. I stood alone with Jack in his father's bedroom, the bed and bed frame already gone. It was determined that I would inherit the stereo; as I worked to dismantle it, pulling apart wires, Jack stuffing random leftover items into bags, I tried not to look over my shoulder at the irregular hole in the far wall.

Sometimes I wonder if her father's sudden death didn't prepare Stacy, on some level, for our lives capsizing this completely. It is a shameful thought, one I try to squirm away from as it hits me, but drowning quietly in my own rage and despair, I am unable to escape it.

One night after dinner, when we have

relocated to the couch, I lower the volume on the music because I don't want distractions. I turn to her; I have a question.

"Before Greta died, did you think the world was"—I hesitate and think of my promise to my unborn one—"a good, safe place?"

She looks at me with surprise, sensing the weight of my need.

"Huh. That's a hard one." She furrows her brow, her words emerging slowly: "I think moments in my life . . . made me assume horrible things just **happen**," she said. "Maybe before the accident, I assumed we were safe from some of those horrible things. But no. When Greta died, I didn't have a worldview that was shattered."

As she says this, I feel the embarrassing truth curdle inside my gut. **I would have said yes.** The naïveté of this belief sears me now, fills me with self-loathing that is almost blinding. I might have hemmed and hawed, qualified, but I would have said yes. This is the scream living in me, I realize. This version of me—this contemptibly happy and thoughtless child—has been mauled. He vomits blood, paws the blacktop with curled fingers, but grotesquely refuses to die.

"I feel like the brick hit me, too," I mutter to Stacy. "It didn't kill me all the way, and now there's this voice inside of me that's always screaming. I need this guy inside of me to stop screaming."

✧

We begin thinking about names, but all of our research feels haunted, a funhouse-mirror reminder of our first giddy go-round.

"Aurora is the name of a Roman goddess who turned tears to morning dew," I offer.

Stacy winces.

"It's hard to say, isn't it? Aw-**roh**-ruh. Nice meaning, though."

"Hope?" Stacy asks.

"Might be a lot to burden a kid with."

"Yeah, maybe too literal," Stacy concedes, adding thoughtfully, "I knew a nice woman named Hope in high school."

"How about Renata? It means 'reborn.'"

Stacy frowns: " 'Reborn' is weird."

Edith. Ida. Jesse. Owen. Rose?

"We can't have a 'Rose Greene.'"

"How about Francis?"

"I can't tell if there's something . . . smarmy about the name Francis," says Stacy. I cannot rebut this, so on we go.

With fear and trauma still ringing so loudly in our ears, we can't fully believe in the child growing in Stacy's belly; it is a possibility on the horizon, a good thing that might pan out. That little white life-cloud on the sonogram is more like a sun: I can't stare at it directly for too long. I talk to the cloud, imagine it shifting into a being. I imagine that I can hear its mind start to whir. It knows me, I think. **I know,** I whisper to it. **Daddy will fix his heart. I know.**

I try to meditate. I envision my crippling rage and pain as clouds passing over a constant sky; I imagine myself as a blood cell passing through an artery, just an agent of movement. I try, in other words, to pretend to be something other than human, maybe one of those stone Buddhas with the downcast eyes and smile playing across their lips. This is meant to be the look of perfect detachment and inner peace. It strikes me now as awfully smug.

I find sentences I hate in articles I read to escape. "Experts Predict Zika Mosquitoes Will Be in U.S. by Summer," **The New York Times** announces, coupled with an illustration of a mosquito resembling an agent of mechanized warfare, its body filling with scarlet liquid. The article shows up in my Facebook feed just below a clip of Lin-Manuel Miranda's speech for his win at the 2016 Grammys. "Sebastian, Daddy's bringing home a Grammy for you," he cries exuberantly. I regard him sourly, this beaming representative for a nation of parents and their safe, healthy, growing children.

Another one, this time from The New **Yorker:** a neuroscientist has demonstrated that "a pregnant woman's experience of trauma and PTSD may affect her child's development in the womb. And a study at the University of Zurich has shown that stress in a male mouse can alter the RNA in his sperm, causing depression and behavioral changes that persist in his progeny." The mantra coursing beneath the surface haunts me: **You are not the same. You are both damaged.**

I watch a racist—an ignorant and malevolent man who believes in nothing—slowly rise to power. I watch people punching protesters at his rallies, and I note the year of his ascent. "Imagine all this happening today! In 2016!" I hear people say over and over again. No one can understand it—this simply can't be happening. People aren't this dumb or this cruel.

I keep my mouth shut mostly, but I think: **Of** course **they are.** Having my daughter die in such meaningless circumstances has permanently altered my sense of human possibility, it seems, changed my understanding of our potential and capability. We are a difficult, ungovernable species, forever staving off chaos with one hand and succumbing to it with the other. We aren't here long enough to stop fighting death, to relax into our existence and gaze clearly. We thrash, mostly blindly, from one pole of oblivion to another. We are lucky if we truly notice three or five things in between. The rest is shouting, or being shouted at, or hiding underneath a blasted scrap from a raging storm.

✧

It's a boy. Our nurse helpfully points out the size of his testicles during the sonogram. They are swollen, we learn, by amniotic fluid. We both laugh about her remarks after, but it underlined our surprise, to be handed a new model of being. A boy. **Our** boy. We settle on the name Harrison, like George, the spiritual seeker of the Beatles, or Lou Harrison, the bearded composer and West Coast mystic. Or, Stacy adds, flashing me a sly look, like Harrison Ford.

I have heard his heartbeat again, a miraculous fact, a magic trick I thought unrepeatable. My own heart is painfully swollen, inflamed—I am full to bursting with pain, with joy, with regret, with anger, with bitterness, with wonder, with awe. He is invisible to me, but he is there.

I sense some sort of metaphysical authority shining his unforgiving flashlight in my panicked face. He hands me a summons with a terse flourish: **OK, you've got twenty more weeks to get your shit together.** He pauses meaningfully, finding my eyes from underneath the brim of his hat. **You got that, Daddy? Get your shit together.**

✧

We are first-timers at a local grief group. A round-faced man with a jowly smile and a frizzy halo of hair greets us amiably. "I'm Alec," he says unnecessarily, his name tag staring at us from his right breast pocket. I take his hand, and then he takes Stacy's. As he does, he catches and holds us with his gaze. He has an effortless warmth, a comfort that seems forever at the surface, not something he has to turn on. I feel both of us lean toward him like heliotropic plants, open up slightly. **This is what a support-group lifer feels like,** I think. My mother's first husband, after he went through AA, emitted a similar frequency.

Alec lost a sister, he informs us easily. "You guys are going to want to go around the corner to the main room," he says, pointing us in the right direction.

We enter the main conference room, hanging back at the entrance for a moment to watch. There is a pleasant sort of shabbiness to everything—the pebbly-looking old rug; the fluorescent overhead light, which makes us all look pale and unhealthy; the table, at the far end, with the requisite grocery-store cookies, the two thermoses with coffee and tea. The long-term members are gathered in small circles, and you can read in their body language, like they were in their own kitchen, that they'd been doing this for years. They talk too quietly for me to hear what is being said, but their faces are open, warm, relaxed.

"Welcome," a tall, lanky, middle-aged man says, looming suddenly in front of me. He, too, holds out his hand, which appears at the end of a very long, bony arm. "I'm so sorry to meet you under these circumstances, but I'm glad you came," he says, his voice deep and thrumming like a cello. "My name is Jake. I lost my daughter Renee twelve years ago to cancer. She was twenty-four."

The entire room constricts, and there is only Jake in front of me.

"I am so sorry to hear it, Jake," I tell him, gripping his hand back and trying to block out everyone around him as I focus on his face. "My daughter, Greta, died ten months ago. She was two." Jake's hand remains loose, his eyes calm and sorrowful on mine.

"I'm sorry, Jayson," he says, reading my name tag. He gestures to the room with his free hand. "You've come to a good place here."

Stacy and I have been meaning to come to this group for some months. Our natural reticence kept us away, but we have been talking at home lately about our need to "integrate" our healing, our grief, into our daily lives. This is how we talk about our grief now: earnestly, like it is a school project of Greta's she needs help with. Since learning the sex of our son, I have shared my vision of the traffic cop, handing me a court summons for the due date. Stacy admits she is also hearing the clock tick louder: "We have to make room for him while figuring out how to honor Greta," she says sensibly. I do not know how she has figured this out so thoroughly, as usual, but I can only agree and be grateful. So we are here.

"Here," for reasons I do not understand, is a Sunday-school classroom. Because this is our first meeting, we are to be kept apart from the others, many of whom have been coming to the meetings for decades. It's as if our fresh pain might be contagious and we need to be quarantined. But this means that everywhere we look, we see the results of arts and crafts projects done by little hands. **Surely there was another space available?** I think as I crane my neck to look at two purple handprints, aged five.

Judy, the moderator, is coming to meet us. I look around at the other first-timers. I wonder what kind of dark energy we emit, if there is a thermal map for this kind of sadness—would we glow like a small city, this gathering of ten or twelve people in a back room?

We sit around in awkward silence, unsure if we are allowed to speak to one another yet. After a minute, Judy walks in, sits down, brushes off her pant legs briskly, and fixes us with a practiced "no bullshit" stare.

"Someone just told me I am too aggressive," she announces by way of introduction. She shrugs theatrically, her eyelids low: "Ask me if I care."

I can feel myself drawing inward, shielding

my vital organs from her. I don't want to be in a room with her right now, with Stacy and my son and the memories of my daughter.

Judy introduces herself. Her daughter died twenty years ago, and she has been a moderator for many years. "What happened to us is different from other kinds of loss," she says. "It just is. Everyone else thinks they can help you, but the truth is there is no one on Earth that understands the way we feel. People are going to try to comfort you; they probably have already tried. But there are no words for this path, and no one who hasn't experienced this kind of loss will be able to say anything to help. We have experienced the worst affliction that can happen in a lifetime, and **no one understands how we feel.**"

She stops and takes in the room, determining if we have soaked up her point. She nods imperceptibly, moving forward.

"For years after, all I felt was anger—such anger," she says, shaking her head slightly. "I wrote pages and pages of nothing but anger and despair, the things I felt. And then, when it was all out of me"—here she mimics washing her hands of it—"I locked it in a drawer. I never wanted to see or read any of it again.

"When I found this place, I started to learn that maybe all the things that were going on in my head weren't so crazy after all," she continues. "Maybe there were some other people who felt like this, too. This is a safe place for people like us, where we can be together. Now, why don't we start by going around the room, and each of you share what brought you here today?"

Counterclockwise around the room, our mute mourners break their silence one at a time. Ann, whose forty-year-old son collapsed and died of a seizure, midsentence, right in front of her. Lydia, the woman across from me, who lost her teenage son to a drug overdose. Today was Tuesday; he had died the previous Thursday. I gaze at her in wonder, at her presence of mind to be here. She sits tranquil, quiet. Her eyes are soft and watery, but she does not cry. She is flanked by two friends, who seem to be ready to steady her should her composure wobble. She tells her story simply and gracefully, and the circle moves on.

The circle lands on Stacy before it lands on me, so she clears her throat softly. "Well, we are here because our daughter, Greta, died about ten months ago, when she was two years old," she begins. "There was . . . some falling masonry . . ."

I squeeze my hands between my thighs in empathy; the story is still such a hard one to tell, mostly because no one seems to understand it. Stacy picks up the thread again, plowing ahead.

"She was sitting on a bench in front of a building on the Upper West Side with my mom, when a piece of the windowsill fell. She never woke up; they did surgery to reduce the swelling in her brain but it was too late. It was such a freakish accident, so random. Sometimes it's hard to—"

Judy, to our surprise, cuts in here, interrupting Stacy midsentence. "You see? You see? Chaos! It's pure chaos. The world is a shooting gallery, and we all got hit."

Eyes wide, I glance over at Stacy, who looks stricken. **Do you think she was supposed to cut you off telling your story? Is a group leader supposed to do that?** I sense

Stacy, feeling rebuked, receding back into the wall. I try to take a breath and unclench my jaw and find it only clenches tighter. I count backward in my head from ten and lose it at seven, and the circle continues to my right.

The couple next to us looks to be a few years younger. Their son emerged stillborn; there had been no warning signs. The husband just holds his wife's hand, silent.

I look at Judy for guidance, only to find that she, alarmingly, is choking up. "You know, your story is really one that gets to me," she says.

I get angrier, and I have an ominous foreboding I will soon say something I will regret. **Is she comparing our stories? Is a group moderator supposed to do** that?

"There's something about being robbed of your future"—I stifle a gasp, and I feel Stacy stiffen at my side—"that is particularly terrible." My sense of certainty grows—I am about to be angry in a very inappropriate setting and in a very small room. Then she actually says it: "At least everyone else here got to have a relationship with their child and got to know them."

"Not when she was two years old," I mumble, just loud enough for half the room to hear me.

Judy, however, does not. The discussion churns ahead, oblivious to my smoldering. There is another woman from the main group, a lifer, who has been brought in to help guide us in addition to Judy. Her name is Carolyn. Judy turns to Carolyn now: "Carolyn, tell me about Jordan."

Carolyn makes a florid gesture of helplessness with her left hand, waving it limply in the sky like a silent-movie damsel. Then the hand falls, forgotten, to her lap, while her other comes up unconsciously to rest at a chunky piece of costume jewelry at her neck.

"What is there to say?" she asks. She stares hungrily at the spot just in front of her, as if her son might materialize and help her find words. "He was . . . **everything**. He was endlessly creative; he was fierce; he was hilariously funny. He was . . ." Carolyn glances quickly up to the foam tiles in the ceiling. "He was pure light.

"I am surrounded by his things now, in

my house," she adds, still looking up. "I have many people telling me to get rid of some of it, but he was just so creative . . . he made so many things, paintings and sculpture and textile. How could I ever get rid of any of it? I am comfortable living with the pieces of my Jordan."

Carolyn looks down and scans the room, her face darkening slightly. "Jordan's wife has remarried." Her face is sour. "She has a new family. She doesn't understand why I want to live with all of her dead husband's **things**." She enunciates the last word with a bite of accusation. "She seems to have **moved on**."

She glowers at this, then turns plaintive. "Everyone expects me to move on at some point," she says sadly, appealing to us. "I don't want to move on. Why would I? I've never understood why people think that. Sometimes I ask them, 'Why should I move on?' They never have an answer for me."

Here she lapses into silence again, her hand still resting on her necklace. I wonder if Jordan made it.

"We are, all of us here, on the other side of

a great wall," she concludes. "Everyone else is over there. We can hear them, and they can hear us, but we can never join them again."

"I know what you mean about the wall," I say hesitantly, breaking my silence. "But I don't want to live on this side of it forever. I'm really scared of being stuck over here. My therapist reassures me I'm not stuck, but I feel like I've been cycling through the same two stages of grief, over and over—some kind of acceptance and then this blinding anger, back and forth."

"That's a common misconception," chimes in the woman to Lydia's left, speaking for the first time. "The stages of grief aren't linear. Just because you're angry again doesn't mean you've somehow gone **backward**."

I nod absently as I take a tissue. Lydia's friend seems versed in the language of therapy sessions.

"The stages!" Judy shrieks. "God help me with the stages." She regards Lydia's friend coolly, eyes narrowing: "You're a therapist, aren't you?"

The woman nods, her composure unruffled. Judy looks satisfied at the unmasking.

"I thought so," she says. "You know, normally we have a rule, we say no professionals are allowed"—she pounces on the word "professionals" to make the scare quotes absolutely, fingernails-on-blackboard   unmistakable— "at our meetings." She leans forward a little more, as if conspiratorial: "Since you are her friend and you are accompanying her, though, we'll make an **exception**."

Her posture and tone resemble a mob boss softening up a mark—**I like you, Eddie**— just before snuffing him out. Stacy and I stare at each other for a moment: Was this really happening?

"So you are a therapist then," pipes in Carolyn. "Maybe you can answer a question for me, about this 'acceptance' business. Why would I want to 'accept' my son's death?"

"It's not about accepting his death so much as learning to live with it and accepting it as reality," Lydia's friend replies, her therapist game face on. "No one asks you to accept that it is somehow OK."

"Well, how is that **acceptance** then?" demands Judy. Her elbows are on her knees now, chin jutting. She and Carolyn have identified the intruder, and I feel them circling her like antibodies. "I refuse to accept what happened to my child. I will not accept it until the day I die. I accept that it **happened** . . ."

"Well, maybe that's just another word for it then, but that's semantics," the therapist friend says. She's a little less smooth now, a little more heated, and I can sense her mentally rolling up her sleeves. She has some skin in the game. Next to her, her newly bereaved friend sits quietly, her hands in her lap, like she might during an argument at the family dinner table.

The room is devolving swiftly, and I clear my throat nervously. "I'm sorry I brought up the stages," I say, raising a hand. A few discomfited laughs. "I think what I meant is that for me, they've been a helpful map. They don't make sense for everyone, necessarily"— I make a gesture of inclusion to Judy and Carolyn—"but for me, it's helped to have a spot on the map. When I'm angry—"

"When you're angry, just **be angry**," Judy cuts in. "You don't need to label things."

My anger turns cold, and I wheel on her. Suddenly I feel somewhat dangerous to myself. "Could you let me **finish**?" I say loudly, not caring how hostile I sound. "I really don't appreciate you cutting me off while I am talking. Or, for that matter, when my wife is."

I see Judy's eyes refocus on me then, and her jaw sets. My foreboding becomes prophecy: I am about to get into a fight with the moderator of a grief support group.

"Look," she says. "I can tell you are struggling with anger. I did, too. But I never claimed to be perfect. I'm just another bereaved parent like you. The only difference is I've been on this road a little longer than you have."

"I can't believe you would say that," I say, raising my voice. "What gives you the right to **pull rank on someone** with your grief?"

Now the entire room is my audience, mine and Judy's, our angers flaring and competing for the remaining oxygen in the room. We are the two trolls in this group, she and I, and we openly glare with recognition at each other. The other parents, the stories and grief they bore with them into that room, become as remote to me as natural disasters in other countries.

After a moment, Judy seems to realize how inappropriate it is to be arguing with a first-time member. I watch her adjust and modulate. "I'm sorry if you took offense at something I said," she says, landing somewhere just left of apologizing.

"It's OK," I say, with a tone meant to convey just how fucking far from OK it is.

Someone else cuts in uncomfortably and the group moves on, but for me the rest of the meeting occurs on mute, drowned out by the pounding in my ears.

After, Judy comes up to me, attempting to smooth over the rift. She pulls another nearby member into our circle, laughing theatrically: "Boy, let me tell you, this guy got the full Judy tonight!" She shakes her head. "You know what happened?" addressing me by talking to her friend. "There was a **professional** in the room"—there's that word again, and it occurs to me that this is also a common euphemism for "whore"—"and I just got a little feral."

She grips my shoulders and looks me in the eyes, and I feel myself tense up again. "Promise me something? Promise me you'll come back. Every single time is different. Different members, different"—and here she pauses, her eyes searching mine—"moderators. That's all I've got to say. Don't make this be your only shot."

I mutter something stiffly to her. I am unwilling to accept decency and grace from this woman, now that I've invested energy in making her my enemy.

I puncture the silence of the long subway ride home a few stops in. "I'm sorry I got into a fight with the grief group lady," I mumble, hot and ashamed.

"I saw that coming a mile away," Stacy replies drily.

✧

Stacy and I are flying to New Mexico to be with our daughter's spirit. It is a place we have no memories of, either apart from each other or as a family. In this, as in everything else on our path toward healing, we have no idea what we are doing.

The accident happened a mere twenty days after Greta's second birthday; somewhere in there, Mother's Day came and went. These

260 ONCE MORE WE SAW STARS

twenty days are a haunted landscape, and our memories of her start churning up so bright and vivid they begin to seem unreal. "Sometimes my memories of her feel like folklore in my own brain," Stacy says. What about the time Greta looked up from her plate and said, out of the blue, "Food is very special to me"? Stacy was at home with her and I was at work, and she texted me, thunderstruck. Now the story has started to seem blurry and unreliable: There's no way Greta actually **said** that, did she? When two grief-stricken parents are the only witnesses, the details start to feel suspect. And yet I have the text message in my history, dated and time-stamped.

We are spending a few days in Santa Fe and then driving into Taos, a small artist community that doesn't so much border the mountains as taper off gradually into them. Somewhere in those foothills is Golden Willow Retreat, an adobe house on a patch of farmland run by a man named Ted Wiard. Ted has the sort of grief story that could make anyone feel faint: in short succession, he lost his brother to a boating accident, his wife to cancer, and then his two children to a car crash. Dazed and lost, he checked himself briefly into a rehab program, simply because he could not find anywhere else to go. Then he returned to his home of Taos and built a center of his own, a resting place for those in deep grief.

This is where we plan to wake up on our daughter's third birthday. We are both intensely curious about the place and a little apprehensive, as we were before Kripalu, about the unknown it represents—we can't even find any pictures of it online. We have never celebrated Greta's birthday without her, so we are flying double blind.

Our first evening in Santa Fe, we dress up in warm, festive clothes and go wandering. The first meal we eat is covered in green chilies, and we decide that henceforth every meal we eat will be covered in the same. Then we meander, sated and content, to a new age bookstore and crystal shop. We spend a befuddled hour or so in there, picking up crystals and inspecting them as if we are waiting for them to do something to us.

"How about this one?" I ask Stacy. "It's self-healing Inca quartz."

"Ooh, I like that one," Stacy says, looking. She inspects the price tag: $250. We put it back.

I spend twenty minutes gazing at the books in the back; I walk past EASTERN THOUGHT, browse with some mild interest in WICCAN. I see the names of writers I vaguely recognize: Alan Watts, Harold S. Kushner. I find myself thumbing through a copy of the Bhagavad Gita, a seven-hundred-verse Hindu scripture. **Probably a little too far in the deep end**, I think. When Stacy comes to find me later, I am holding a Tibetan singing bowl up to my ear, tracing its edges with the wooden stick and listening. I give Stacy a lost look: **Do I need** this? We start laughing together in the middle of the store. We leave clutching two small stones, one for each of us, having spent about fifteen dollars and feeling reasonably secure in our purchases. "We have to start small," Stacy reasons. "Baby steps!"

We go hiking in astonishing rock formations, the kinds that have earned the Southwest its mythical status. I have spent plenty of time in mountains before, visiting family in Colorado, but it's true that something here feels different. It could be the supreme absence of other people, or the twisting and alien nature of the formations themselves. Or maybe there is something to the state motto, the one on key chains and souvenir-store tchotchkes, deeming this the "Land of Enchantment." I don't feel Greta's presence yet, but I feel Stacy's, warm and clear, beside me, and I feel the presence of our son.

The day we drive into Taos, we stop at a café at the edge of the small town, with murals painted on the walls by a local artist. There is a rusted old Harley parked out front, next to a VW with a COEXIST bumper sticker. They are playing some indie rock in here I should recognize but can't place. I look out the window and try to imagine what it will be like to be alone with our thoughts for the next several days and how we are going to pass the time. The mountains are visible from the café window. **Will we find you here, baby girl?** I wonder. We get back in the car and drive farther into nothingness, only the occasional roadside memorial in the form of a cross to mark distance.

The first turn off the country highway that

our GPS alerts us to takes us down a dirt road and around trailers, as we drive essentially through their backyards. The road angles up and off to the left suddenly, and as we round the corner, an abandoned house looms, coated in graffiti and with all its windows knocked out, presumably shattered by bored kids hurling rocks. "Well, I hope this isn't it," I say to Stacy. It's not, and we keep driving.

The road keeps tugging us up, our rental car straining like a vintage roller coaster cresting the first drop. A few small houses, front drainage ditches nearly choked by weeds, pass by, and the road narrows so suddenly that a mailbox jutting into the road nearly knocks our mirror. Suddenly a field opens up on our right, and Golden Willow unfolds before us. The house sits at a comforting remove in the middle of a vast field, flanked at its back by a small adobe chapel, the only two buildings in the treeless plain.

We stand outside our car for a moment, the wind whipping into us, unsure whether we should knock, fearful we might interrupt another griever in the midst of some cathartic revelation. Stacy calls the administrator,

Kiersten, from the driveway, only to watch her emerge, phone in hand, from the door. She hugs us both and invites us in.

Ted is out of town, at a conference of some sort, for the entire time we are here, but his presence hovers everywhere. Everyone seems to have been touched in some way by him, and everyone here has a story. The woman who cooks meals taught his children at school. Kiersten alludes to rough times of her own, years ago, as a midwife. "Ted was there," she says simply.

On the day of Greta's birthday we are scheduled to meet with someone named Jim, a therapist who works at Golden Willow as a "ceremonialist." Much like Maureen the medium, Jim the ceremonialist is the subject of intense speculation between Stacy and me.

When he arrives, we are alone in the house except for Kiersten, who's in the office. He knocks on the door; I answer. He wears a fringed white buckskin vest, and his white hair is pulled back into a ponytail. He has a hound's tooth around his neck, and his face and hands are brown and craggy like the surrounding rocks. He smells overwhelmingly of tobacco; when I shake his hand, the scent fills my nostrils.

Jim's skin is sunbaked and geologic, and it is difficult to tell if he is in his forties or his sixties. He speaks slowly, unhurriedly, like someone who judges the hour by the sun. "I know a lot of different ceremonies," he says, picking something absently off his buckskin vest with a leathery, calloused hand and flicking it off. "It all depends on what sort of . . . experience you two are looking for." He looks us in the eyes. "What are you looking for?"

And there it is: the million-dollar question neither of us can answer. This is really new to us, we try to explain. We are feeling our way toward a more spiritual life. We've both had some experiences that have made us want to connect to deeper things. We are not religious. But, you know.

Jim cuts in to save us. "I think I have an idea," he says. "I'm going to go out to the chapel to set up; you two can just wait here. I'll come and get you."

And with that, he lumbers out of the room, picking up a sack at his feet. We watch him open the sliding glass doors and make his way across the field to the chapel.

"What do you think he's doing out there?" Stacy whispers.

"I have no idea." I'm whispering, too, even though we are alone in the room. "What do you think we're going to walk in on? I just hope Jim isn't naked."

We snicker like middle schoolers; we've traveled thousands of miles, and somehow even this far along in our journey we revert to behaving like little kids when confronted with the unfamiliar. I think of Greta again, her little toes in the ocean, flinching a little from the ferocity before her. **I know how you feel, little girl.**

Just then, a loud thud makes us both jump. "Jesus!" I say involuntarily. Something has slammed, hard, into the far window, and I look over only to see a smear and a single feather. The sound is loud enough that Kiersten emerges from the back office.

We walk over to the window and find ourselves looking at a single grey dove, stone dead and on its back, its black eyes fixing on us sightlessly. No one speaks.

I break the silence. "That probably happens a lot, right?"

Kiersten is still looking at the bird. She turns to us, a quizzical smile on her face. "No, actually. That never happens."

I laugh nervously. "That doesn't seem like a good sign," I joke.

"I don't think it's good or bad," Kiersten says. "It's now part of your journey. I'm going to go bring it to Jim."

She steps outside and scoops up the bird's corpse with her bare hands, marching over to the chapel. Jim steps out (still fully clothed, I am relieved to note), and the two of them confer. Kiersten says something; Jim nods, looking down thoughtfully at the bird. Finally, he takes it with him into the chapel and closes the door. Kiersten brushes her hands together a little, heads back toward the house. She looks at us meaningfully again when she reenters the kitchen, not saying anything, and then heads back in the office, the door closing behind her.

Stacy and I are spooked into silence; the dead dove has robbed us of the luxury of skepticism. Maureen's voice comes back to me from Kripalu: **Pay attention to signs.** Well, this didn't feel like a sign; this felt like an intervention. Whatever is happening to us right now feels undeniable, outside of our comprehension. We have waded in over our heads. Whatever happens next we have no choice but to embrace.

Finally, Jim comes out to get us. "I think we're all ready now," he says simply. We follow him wordlessly over the rock path out the back and into the small chapel. Ted built it himself with the help of a group of teenagers and young children in the area who had lost siblings or parents.

There is a small fire in the woodstove. At the far end, we spot a series of symbols and totems on the floor, arranged in a circle. Jim sits down, cross-legged, and we follow suit. There is a bag of fresh tobacco next to him, a slit cut open in its side, and a series of small patches of cloth, laid out in a cross formation. "This is a tobacco prayer-tying ceremony," he explains, gesturing at the cloths. "Each color represents a different direction: black for the west, red for the north, yellow for the east, and white for the south."

Each of those directions has different emotional connotations, he explains. He palms a cloth and expertly pinches a handful of tobacco with his fingers and places it in the center, folding the edges and twisting everything into a little parcel. "When you hold the tobacco between your fingers, you try and take a moment to focus on it. The idea is to imbue it with an intention." He loops twine around the top of the parcel, pulls it taut: "You choose the color that speaks to you, and you put the tobacco inside it."

I feel certain that I am going to spill tobacco bits all over the chapel floor. But with shaky hands, I pluck a purple cloth, between east and west—the realm of the great unknown, Jim says, the great mystery of life and death—and hold a hairy strand of tobacco between my thumb and forefinger. I stare at it, hard: **I want to be at peace with where you are, Greta,** I think to it, and I try to imagine the thought being soaked up into the leaves from the oils of my fingers. I gently press the tobacco into the bundle and tie it off. It lists to the side, slightly, but it holds. My prayer is intact.

The three of us fold and tie silently for some time. When we have each made four or five packets, all tied on a long piece of twine, we stop and compare.

"The yellow is for our son," Stacy says, holding up her string, which shows red, yellow, black, and white packets. "He feels like a new, uncomplicated energy to me, for some reason . . . very eager, very open and happy. This is an intention to be ready for him and to be ready to receive his energy."

At the end of the ceremony, Jim gets up to go and then remembers something. Going over to the corner, he unveils the still corpse of the dove, wrapped in a blanket. Then he pulls out a pocketknife, flicks open the blade, and places the tip at the joint connecting the wing to the bird's torso. He hesitates and looks up at us: "Is this too weird?"

I start laughing in spite of myself. "I really don't know, Jim. What does 'too weird' mean in these circumstances?"

He laughs back, a rumbly smoker's sound. "Good point."

He begins sawing. The cartilage shifts, and Jim has to pull the joint taut. The operation is not graceful; the knife is dull, and he has to work hard enough to make me wince. But after a minute, Jim presents us each with a cut-off dove's wing, the edges still glistening pink. "You're probably going to want to put those in salt," he advises.

We exit the chapel, Stacy and I holding a bloodied wing each. Some cumulus clouds, shocking in their three-dimensional clarity, have moved overhead. We are holding our prayer ties, which we will burn on our last day, sending our hopes and fears and intentions into the air. Jim digs a small hole with a shovel, while we stand off to the side. He lowers the wingless dove into the hole, scatters some tobacco, and makes a cross sign of sorts, an invocation toward the north, south, west, and east. "Thank you to the Great Spirit for sending us this messenger," he intones gravely. "We wish you peace on your journey."

He stands, brushes his knees off, and looks at us, suddenly Jim the therapist again, his shamanic air shaken off.

"Well, that's it," he says. He cocks his head. "If you found this helpful and want to do something more, you can just let Kiersten know. I'd be happy to come back. If not, I hope you took some healing from this experience."

And with that, he turns and walks back to the house. We are alone with our thoughts, the interred bird beneath our feet.

Stacy breaks the silence. "I'd like him to come back."

✧

The next morning, we are visited by a body worker named Hannah. I go first, and as she sets up her massage table, I tell her about the dove.

"It was dark and funny in a way that made me think of Greta," I say. "She had a slapstick sense of humor, and she loved it when we were flustered. It cracked her up. A dove smacking into a window and scaring the shit out of us—it felt like the kind of signal she would send."

"I'm sure it was," Hannah murmurs, kneading my shoulders. Then she puts a hand to my chest and flinches slightly, as if it were a hot stove. She takes in a short breath and whispers, "She's **right here**."

She laughs with wonder, her palm softening. My grief pumps out of me, like a broken water main.

"Oh, Jayson, I'm so sorry," she says. "I know this might make you sad to hear, but you can never really be alone. She's right here inside you. It's remarkable. **Right here**." She traces a circle around my right clavicle and breastbone. "Was she here?"

"Right after she was born," I whisper.

After Hannah leaves, we wander the grounds, feeling pliant, suggestible. The dove, the chapel, the solitude—we feel cracked open somehow, ready for wherever else Jim might bring us. We wander to the back fence to pet the two old, watery-eyed donkeys that live on the grounds. We do yoga in the chapel. We wait for Jim to return.

When he arrives again at the house later that afternoon, he is carrying nothing but a drum.

"I'm going to lead you on a spirit journey," he announces, sitting down with the drum between his knees, tracing a line around the stretched skin. "I can't say for certain what you will encounter, but I can tell you a number of things that some people experience. You may come into contact with a spirit animal; you may be visited by other visions. Some of them might be frightening or vivid, but the important thing to remember is not to be afraid. Sometimes the spirit animal overwhelms you; it might even move to touch you. It's important not to flinch from that, because whatever it wants to do for you is healing. It may even appear violent, but your spirit animal never wishes you harm. If they move to touch you, it is safe to embrace them; they are offering you healing, and it is medicine they bring.

"The other thing to remember is that you will trip over the conscious mind along the way," he says. "It is part of the journey as well. As you go further into yourself, your conscious mind attempts to pull you out of the spirit realm at every step. You might start to fidget, become more aware of your body again, or have an impulse to move your legs, or to remember the room around you. This is all normal, and the best thing you can do when this happens is to just acknowledge it and let it go. You can keep going inward."

Stacy lies on the couch; I choose the floor, just beneath the skylight. When I close my eyes, the sunlight turns the landscape behind my eyelids white. Jim starts to beat the drum, rhythmically and deliberately, the cadence of raindrops from a gutter. The light expands behind my eyelids and gathers depth, and suddenly the currents of light become a flitting shape: a butterfly. I see wings, fluttering unmistakably. They are diaphanous, light passing through their webbing. My conscious mind hiccups in disbelief, right on cue, and the butterfly dissolves, bringing the room and the floor and my arms and legs back into focus, but Jim's drum keeps beating, and as my breathing slows, it reappears. It flutters above me, circles, and lands on my chest. If it were possible for a butterfly to arch an eyebrow, that is what it does to me. **Well, come on,** it seems to say, playful and expectant.

It lifts off my chest, and I follow it, watching the slow flexing of its wings as they expand. Suddenly, they are no longer butterfly wings;

they are eagle wings, broad and strong and spreading for miles in both directions. There is wind in my face, and I look down, seeing my hands clutching the eagle's broad shoulder blades. We are soaring high above miles of forest, trees passing below in a blur. The eagle dives and the forest floor rears up before me. I tumble weightlessly off its back and into a wide, open field. Lying there, sinking into the earth beneath me and with grass blades tickling my fingers and grazing my ears, I gaze up at the blue sky.

Greta walks up. She is wearing the white denim jacket she was wearing the day before the accident, when she and Grandma Suz went to the park. **Hi, Daddy,** she says, silently. **Hey, little girl,** I say. I stand up at her beckoning and follow her to the edge of the forest, where the trees get thicker. The eagle reappears, and I mount its shoulders; for some reason, I am unable to follow Greta's weaving little white dot of a body through the trees without its help.

The eagle slows where Greta has stopped, at a massive pit of earth. I stand at the lip with her, looking into it. There is a humid, loamy smell emanating from the bottom, a scent that hints at unknown things. I can't see more than ten feet down and I shrink from the edge; I am afraid. But Greta looks at me, wrinkling her nose in that funny smile of hers, and off she goes, scrabbling down the side. I have no choice but to follow her down, into the very center of the earth. It only gets cooler the farther down we go, and I can barely make out her jacket as she moves eagerly ahead of me.

We meet at the very bottom, the surface invisible. The dirt down here breathes. Greta kneels down to it and, with her two small hands, scoops up rich, living earth, letting it stream from her palms as she holds it up to me: **See? See?** She looks at me meaningfully, and I understand: when I returned to the earth, Greta would be literally everywhere. Her love and presence would blanket me. She would be flowers, bees, sky, roots, dirt, frogs, water. And so would I. Suddenly we are standing at the lip of the pit again, and then just as suddenly back in the blinding light of the field. Greta has lifted us out somehow, back to the surface. The eagle lands on a branch above me, fixing me with its stern look. Greta, now a tiny figure at the edge of the field, waves sunnily to me. **Good-bye, Daddy,** she says to me, confident and serene in her knowledge that I understood.

And I do; I feel the understanding coursing through my veins, carrying the message with it to every corner of my body. When I die, I will return and sink back into the earth. I lie down in the field again and wait for it to happen. The eagle looms above me, massive, but I am unafraid. I turn my face up to its beak. It pecks out my eyes, drops them in the grass. It tears open my face, spraying blood and pulp and tendons. **Thank you, thank you, thank you,** I whisper to it. I feel the shredding, but there is no pain, just relief as air rushes over the exposed parts of me.

Finally it digs its talons into my chest, closing its claws around my heart. I stiffen and strain, fighting back. I watch the organ lift from my chest cavity, the eagle pulling as it beats its wings upward. But I will not let go: it stays connected to me by hard, stretching tendons, thick like backpack straps. With a grateful sigh, I surrender; the tendons snap, and my beating heart lifts free. The eagle, gripping the bloody thing in its talons, flies up, releasing it at the far edge of the field, where my heart lands with a resounding plop. I am free. My chest cavity withers, plants bloom in my blackening rib cage, and I slowly become earth. I become Greta, and Greta becomes me. The two of us are soil cupped in the palms of the world.

Just then, Jim's drumbeat changes cadence, signaling that it is time to leave this place. The hard yellow eyes of the protector eagle bore into me with a message: **Remember me.** Jim's drum comes to a stop.

"You may now open your eyes," Jim says softly.

My eyes open. Oh, my Greta. My love, my life.

I finally understand.

Six

HARRISON

I CRACK OPEN MY FRONT DOOR, gazing up and down the block. It's eight a.m. and the street is empty: no dogs on leashes sniffing at trees, no neighbors at their mailboxes. I drag cardboard boxes noisily behind me down to the curb. Except for the bus that rumbles past every ten minutes or so, our street is nearly always this quiet—none of our old block's honking minivans, drifting trash, glass shards. I love our new neighborhood, but it's tinged with bitterness. Everywhere I look, there is another place Greta's eyes never saw—walls she never touched, shady swings she never sat in, a wonderful school she will never attend. **You would love it here, Greta,** I tell her.

I make it back inside unnoticed, closing the door behind me with a sigh. My heart is thudding wildly and there are beads of sweat at my temples even though the heat is hours away. It has been eight months since we moved in, but I still fear my new neighbors— their inquisitive smiles, their natural human curiosity. They know nothing of Greta, and I can feel their assumption, from appearances, that we are starting our family, perhaps even newlyweds. I find myself afraid to reinforce this impression or, worse, to correct it. I give them a wide berth as a result, and when I do end up shaking someone's hand, I fight back panic while smiling: **Please don't ask me too many questions.**

I find Stacy awake and bustling in the kitchen, wearing purple underwear and a black tank top. The two items part to bare a slice of pregnant belly, firm as cantaloupe. I kiss her and walk past into our bedroom, stepping around the half-filled open suitcase, our "go bag" list for the hospital— toothpaste, T-shirts, bag of cashews. I add two more items to the mental checklist— deodorant, phone charger—while sliding open the closet door for a fresh shirt.

As I do, the glint of Greta's shrink-wrapped baby clothes catches my eye and I unfocus my gaze. Her clothes are a cube of tightly compressed memories in here, her newborn jammies and her skullcap and all the frilly pink baby clothes we took a single picture of her in before taking them off. Under normal circumstances, we would have passed these on to someone else with a newborn. But now these little outfits are chalk outlines, and to get rid of them would be to surrender more evidence of her existence.

It is mid-August, and late summer clings to us like a musty sheet. Between the weather, the neighbors, and the final days of Stacy's pregnancy, we rarely go outside. Our lives are slowly winding to a halt, and we mostly sit inside together, watching television and trying not to think.

We've begun sorting through these sealed bags again, planting items across the apartment like little warning flags. Stacy has sorted out a few of the unisex outfits and brought them into the living room, where she sits with her coffee. There are some pants in muted purples and greens, some yellow shirts. Next to the scattered baby clothes lies the infant activity mat, dangling stuffed animals and shiny toys. An oil painting of Greta, made for us by a friend, gazes down kindly at us, and at the toys, from the opposite wall. **Do you want us to give all these to your little brother, baby girl?** I ask her silently.

"I had a dream that I was caring for a dog that somehow became a baby," Stacy murmurs next to me to break the silence, and it's only then I notice that she looks troubled. "I picked it up and it was a dog, and then I put it down and it was Greta, and then it was Harrison. There was a boiling pot of hot water next to him. I was just being the most irresponsible mother alive."

There's nothing I can think of to say that doesn't sound pointless to my ears: her dream speaks directly to all of our worst fears.

It is Tuesday. Our son is due in three days. If he keeps to his sister's calendar, born precisely on her due date, he will be in our arms by this weekend.

When he gazes up at us, who is he going to see?

Stacy touches my knee with her left hand. "You should shower and get ready for work," she says softly.

✧

Stacy had a vision at Golden Willow, too. She stood alone in a field, like me. She was greeted not by a butterfly, but by a stag, emerging from the lip of a thick woods. Greta stood next to it, one small hand reaching up to rest lightly at its side. The three of them—Stacy, Greta, the deer—walked through the woods to a clearing, much like the one in my vision, but in Stacy's there were no other animals. There was just a clear pool, its surface undisturbed. Greta beckoned her up to the edge of the water and motioned for her to look out: there, blue and snug and safe, was our son, floating on the surface of the water.

Stacy scanned the edge of the woods for another portent, another sign or visitor, but Greta kept gently bringing her attention back to the baby floating on the pool. Stacy asked her, mutely, what she was meant to do, looking to her for direction. Greta only raised one finger to her lips, looking into Stacy's eyes meaningfully: **Shh**, she said. She pointed again to the water. Then she left.

Driving back from Golden Willow, we

ruminated on what our visions had given us. It was as if my heart were diseased, I ventured—the sickness of my anger, my bitterness, and my self-pity had spread, and the eagle had torn it out of me, organ by organ. The former Jayson who screamed inside of me, the believer in the benevolent universe who had been maimed but not killed by Greta's falling brick, had finally been allowed to perish completely. As the eagle shredded my face, I sensed it was the final obliteration I could not perform on myself. I had wanted to die for so long; now, I finally had.

Stacy, for her part, saw her vision as one about presence, about quietude and calm. "We've been taking care of only ourselves now for so long," she said. "I am going to be a mother again, and that means I have to be ready to give everything I have. Greta was trying to show me how."

Since Greta died, Stacy and I have been asked to live only for each other. Through the blinding nature of our shared pain, we have pulled closer together. We are more tender with each other, less impatient. Now, at the end of another pregnancy, I am acutely aware of the bruising that covers us—how deep the contusions go; how hard all of these spots are about to be pressed again.

Taking care of a child is, if nothing else, an ongoing exercise in self-neglect: You rock a baby until sweat runs down your back. You pick bits of a toddler's leftover food off plates. You fall asleep on bedroom floors, inch away from the crib on your belly, praying your kid doesn't sit up and start screaming again. During the last two weeks, I've tried imagining what it will feel like to exist for someone else again—to be climbed on, yelled at, treated like furniture, regarded as eternal and unmoving, like the sun or the sky. I yearn for the return of this feeling, and I fear what it brings.

Before Greta was born, I tormented myself with an endless series of doomsday scenarios—exhausted, clumsy, I would fall, spinning, in the dark and drop her. Or maybe she would spill something as a toddler while I was making her lunch; I would turn and scream at her. I would see her eyes widen as the fear dawned on her: **Even Daddy can hurt me.**

The truth turned out to be much more complicated. I never dropped Greta, never screamed at her. But we stumbled, raw and half conscious, through our days. Her 4:30 a.m. wake-ups never ceased, and sleeplessness gnawed its remorseless way through our brains. The signs of our exhaustion and inadequacy were everywhere, humiliating us: she wore mismatched clothes and socks on her hands in winter because we couldn't keep her gloves on. We scrambled from work to get to her Brooklyn daycare on time, arriving redfaced and panting. One day, running from the train, I tripped and fell on my carrier bag, feeling my iPad screen crunch beneath me.

When I got home, Stacy was stirring store-bought tomato sauce, which ran in red streaks all over the stove and on the floor. "I dropped it on the floor, but I think I got it in time," she told me, her voice palpable with rising hysteria. "I'm boiling it to make sure." I walked over and glanced in the pot. She had scooped the sauce off our mouse-infested kitchen floor with her hands. I kissed her, suggesting takeout.

We laughed about these moments when we

could. But we were becoming irritable husks of ourselves. When Greta turned eighteen months old, Stacy started taking lactation clients in the evenings after her day's work: "Mommy's gotta go talk to the babies," we would tell her. Greta cried and stomped while Stacy slipped out, stricken and guilty and heartbroken. I would put Greta to sleep and then fight through the cottony blankness of my head to write. We collapsed into bed, barely touching each other.

Things reached a boiling point the week before the accident. The ropes binding our marriage were fraying; we were mean, brittle, short-tempered.

"This will be a good weekend," I promised Stacy. "We'll go out to dinner. We'll sleep in. We just need a reset."

Stacy buried her head in my shoulder; she is a foot shorter than me, so when I hugged her the top of her head met my chin, and I enfolded her completely. "Man, we need a break," she mumbled into me. I could feel her sagging against my frame.

"You're going to go stay overnight at Grandma Suz's this weekend," I reminded

Greta every day that week. She was just getting old enough to comprehend the passing
of days, and we counted them down together.
She knew how to **anticipate** now, I noted.

That Saturday morning, I left Stacy and
Greta alone. I was scheduled to work my
monthly shift at our local food co-op, a
quirky Brooklyn institution where crusty hip-
pie socialists mingled with people like Stacy
and me, who just liked the produce. My job,
that morning, was line director: I stood on a
footstool, waving shoppers on to the checkout counter. It was a ridiculous way to spend
my Saturday morning, but it was only a few
hours. Stacy was driving Greta to the Upper
West Side to drop her off with Susan, and
then we were going to meet for a movie. It
was the beginning of our **reset weekend.**

Forty-five minutes from the end of my
shift, my phone buzzed in my pocket. It was
Stacy, and I answered it to the sound of her
screeching.

"The marathon!" she screamed in my ear.
I could hear her pounding the steering wheel
and faintly discerned Greta wailing in the car
seat behind her. "The Brooklyn marathon is

blocking every street. I can't leave. I've been circling around for forty-five minutes and I'm a mile from home."

I could hear her coming unraveled, and my stomach kicked with visceral anger and frustration.

"I'm sorry," she moaned. "I just don't have this in me right now, OK? I don't. I don't have any reserves at all. I don't know how we're going to get Greta up to my mom's, and I don't know how we're going to get away."

I don't have any reserves, either, but you don't hear me calling you and screaming at you in panic, do you? What gives you the right to do that to me? I snuffed this thought and spoke carefully: "Stacy, calm down. I can't help you do anything when you're this upset. Please just go home and get out of the car. Take Greta to visit Jacob if Saul and Amy are home. When I'm done here, I can shop and come get you. We'll take Greta up on the subway together. Then we'll go to our movie. And then we'll have our weekend. OK?"

Stacy took a shaky breath that I could feel over the phone. "OK. I'm sorry. I didn't mean to lose it. OK."

I walked back, face burning, to resume my post, feeling shaken and exposed.

Our fights, when we had them, were always the same: Stacy would blow up and overreact at small inconveniences, and I would blow up and overreact at her. Both of us would lose our composure, both of us felt foolish as it escalated, and neither of us had a leg to stand on when it was over. "The small things are the big things," she would insist to me, and I agreed with her right up until she got too mad for me to handle, or I got embarrassed and abruptly turned on her. Then we were no longer Jayson and Stacy; we were just two more weary adults miles apart and seething miserably in our mutual failure.

I had a dangerous momentum going by the time my shift ended, hurling moments of her lost temper at her like a prosecutor: **Remember when you said this? Or this? Because I do.**

When we finally met up again, I found her as angry as me.

"Where have you been?" she demanded. "We were supposed to leave an hour ago. Greta's a mess. She's been ready for a nap for

half an hour. She had a total meltdown at
Jacob's house, so that was a nightmare."

I was unready to be the one at fault, and
her anger at me knocked me back a step. I
muttered something defensive, and the two
of us skulked to the subway, Stacy pushing
Greta with the seat reclined. Greta was often
angry with us when we were bickering, but
she was pensive now and just looked up and
smiled that knowing smile of hers.

"I know, sweetheart," I said, ruffling
her hair. "Mommy and Daddy are upset.
We're OK."

The train arrived late and overcrowded,
filled with marathoners wearing their numbers. We forced our miserable way in and
stood there, cramped and not speaking. Then
the train stalled out halfway up Manhattan—
no announcement over the loudspeakers, no
movement. "Oh god, why are we stopped?"
Stacy asked loudly. I felt two sets of nearby
strangers' eyes flick toward us.

Greta squirmed and Stacy reached down to
pull her out of the stroller. Someone cleared
a seat, and she sat on her mother's lap, content once more and making eyes at smiling

passengers. The train moved. We decided to split up once off the train, so that I could take Greta to Susan's and Stacy could run errands. She kissed Greta. She looked at me. "This will get better. Love you."

A block from Susan's, Greta started rocking in her stroller with delight: this street, this light, this smell meant Grandma Suz was near. Seeing her joy, my weariness ebbed, and I pushed her at top speed down the block.

Do you remember when we said goodbye, baby girl? When I dropped you off with Susan, you squirmed out of your stroller and ambled over to the living room. You dumped a small box of rainbow-colored paper clips on the rug and sat down, putting them back one by one in the box. Susan's dog, Margie, barked; Grandma Suz started making you eggs.

"We're all good here, Daddy," Susan said. "Have a wonderful night. You deserve it. Give my love to Stacy." I felt it, then, a muscle released: I relinquished care of you.

I told you to come give me a hug and a kiss. You wandered over and I pulled you close, smelling you, feeling your little hands

pat my back. You gave me a dainty peck and turned away. I stood up, took one last look, and mouthed good-bye to Grandma Suz, who blew me a kiss. I called good-bye one last time. You didn't even look up, waving your hand over your head as I closed the door.

✧

We missed the movie and it was too early for dinner, so we regrouped at a bar. We both felt it then—our weariest and worst selves falling away. Stacy looked at me, her eyes full and pleading, and I felt instantly ashamed.

"I'm sorry," I muttered. Even as I said it, something writhed and kicked in me, some small defiance that refused to settle. I curled my toes and took an unsteady breath and tried again. "I'm sorry."

"I'm sorry, too," Stacy said. "I overreacted, I know. I'm just so tired. Everyone says the first two years are the hardest. But . . . maybe we're finally coming out of the tunnel, you know?"

She reached out and clasped my hand in hers, urgent.

"We have so much to be grateful for," she pleaded. "We have each other; we have Greta. She's **so smart**. I can feel her understanding more and more every day. You can feel that too, right? When we took her to the aquarium, it felt like we were sharing the experience. The fish, the sea lion—she wanted to talk about it the whole way home. She's going to grow so much in the next year. I just . . . this is going to be a good year for us."

The next morning, we slept in until nine. We lay in bed, looking at pictures of Greta. Susan texted us a shot from their morning: Greta had demanded coffee of her own, so Susan gave her one teaspoon of coffee in a mug with milk, and she was tipping it back with gusto. Later on, she told us, they were going to go for a walk in the neighborhood. We should take our time. Stacy and I stretched, luxuriant, in the warmth from the window.

We sat with our coffees, savoring the quiet. We gathered up two big bags of laundry, setting them aside to do later.

"We can still see that movie," I said. "Our last indulgence before we get Greta."

We took our time getting dressed; we wan-

dered out to the elevator, unable to believe
our good fortune.

"I really miss her," Stacy confessed.

I took her hand. "Yeah, me too. It's nice
to miss her, isn't it? We'll see her again soon.
Thank god for Grandma Suz."

"I wonder how they're doing," Stacy said.
She took out her phone. She paused. "Huh."

"What?"

"Oh, I just missed a call from her. That's
odd."

"That **is** odd. Just a call, no text?"

"No text."

"Hmm. Weird. I wonder what she wanted?"
I pulled out my phone. I looked up at Stacy.
I had missed a call from her, too.

❖

A year and three months since that day, and
two days before Harrison is scheduled to
arrive, I take turns talking to both of my children. They seem to be in the same place right
now—one dead, one unborn—which makes
my life on earth feel even more tenuous.
We're right here, Daddy, I keep hearing, but

no matter where I walk, I never find them. There are none of my children here, either, I think rounding every corner.

I'm so sorry, baby girl, I tell her. Your mommy and daddy just needed a weekend. If we hadn't gotten overwhelmed you'd still be here. You have no idea how exhausted I would agree to be to keep you here. Daddy would do anything, give anything, endure anything—Mommy and I could be broke, overwhelmed, tearing each other to shreds with our teeth. Just once more.

Can I tell you a secret, baby girl? I envy you. You are free from time. I can feel time happening to my body now, and it hurts. It stretches me taut like skin over a drumhead. Each minute, hour, passing day, each month, the awareness of all of it accumulating behind and before me. It feels like a sort of dull violence on my heart.

When I was with you in that field, I could feel how free you felt; entire forests rose and fell while we were together. I watched entire mountains rise up from the ground; we were inside one, a couple of faded fossils holding hands embedded in rock. When the eagle took my heart, time is what snapped free.

Eternity sounds comforting. Thank you for teaching me that it exists.

Harrison, I confess you feel unreal to me still, a dream from which I might still wake up. But I have faith that we will find each other. From the first moment your sister appeared to me, popping out from behind that tree in the park, I have been willing to go where you both lead. I am filled with awe at the lessons your sister has taught us; I am ready to receive yours.

✧

On Harrison's due date, Stacy and I eat dinner, both of us in underwear and T-shirts. For some reason, I find myself adopting her dress code as the moment approaches. After dinner, we go for a walk, a nightly ritual. There is a full moon tonight, and we are hoping that it will exert its pull on Harrison.

He spent most of the pregnancy head down, but three weeks ago, Stacy's eyes widened and she gasped in pain midsentence as he suddenly went sideways, then crawled upward until he sat breech, his feet kicking freely at Stacy's bladder and his head in her rib cage.

Like any modern citizen helpless in the face of the unknowable, we googled "how to turn a breech baby" and dutifully performed the rituals. I murmured songs to him, my face at Stacy's belly button, hoping to entice him to swim back down. Stacy did headstands against the wall in our living room; I watched her forehead veins work.

Some of the suggestions seemed so arcane they bordered on witchcraft: I ordered odd, smelly herbs from the internet that were rolled like massive joints; after reading a primer and watching a YouTube video, I lit one, held it to her pinkie toe, and turned it in noncommittal, hesitant circles. "If one of these sites told me to gut an animal, there would be entrails on our rug right now," I joked to her. Was there, finally, nothing we would not embrace headlong in our blind tumble back into parenthood?

One week ago, he rewarded us with a partial turn, and now he lists playfully between six o'clock and three o'clock. That night in bed, I lay my head on her belly and feel feet drumming madly away. Even as his limbs thud at my head, some part of me disbelieves his physical existence; I have seen the outline of him, his head and his rump. But he seems like a thing rather than a person now, an animate part of Stacy. His arms, his face, his beating heart—just thinking about them feels like being fed spotty reports from a dubious source. **Best to wait until we have all the facts,** says some solemn voice inside me. His feet are inches from my face, but when I close my eyes, I only see vast, lapping water, glassy and dark.

✧

Two days pass. Stacy keeps having minor contractions, but they subside. Clara, Danny and Elizabeth's daughter, is going nearly apoplectic with waiting.

"There's been a lot of Harrison-related activity over here," Elizabeth reports drily. "We are writing cards to Harrison, reading books to Harrison, drawing pictures of him. We keep making him unbirthday cakes, and Clara keeps eating them."

We go out to dinner at a pizza place in their neighborhood. Clara has ordered "the Clara," which is in fact just a margherita pizza presented with a conspiratorial, personalized flourish, as if Clara is the only customer granted the privilege. Clara picks up a small slice and hops off her chair to put her hand on Stacy's belly again. "What's he **doing** in there?" she asks, exasperated.

"Every single morning, she runs out of bed yelling, 'Did Harrison come?'" Danny reports. "When I tell her no, she droops and pouts and walks away."

Clara glares at Stacy, suddenly stern: "Tell me the **minute** he starts to come out," she orders.

Stacy hugs Clara, laughing. Clara puts her hand on Stacy's perfectly round tummy, and her eyes widen: "I can feel him, I can feel him!" she squeals. She turns to Danny and Elizabeth: "Mommy, he just kicked my hand!"

Clara looks up again, suddenly serious:

"Even though Greta died, she will still be Harrison's sister, right?"

Clara talks to Greta constantly, makes space for her. She is five, but we have spoken more openly with her about Greta's death than we have most adults, including my therapist. There is something bracing in the clarity of her grief; it is like mountain stream water, free from contaminants like fear, anger, or guilt.

A few months after the accident, we visited Danny and Elizabeth, and Clara pulled out a folder. "Here are all the notes I wrote to Greta at my school," she told us. She took one out, a piece of purple construction paper with a cutout and glued picture of a big dog on it: "Greta, I hope you're having fun in the underworld, not this world," read a note in clear, looping schoolteacher's hand, clearly taking dictation. "P.S. Why do you like dogs so much?"

We made plans with Danny and Elizabeth for when to tell Clara about Harrison. We waited until Stacy was about twenty weeks along; we had them over for dinner, and right before we broke the news, my stomach fluttered with nerves I didn't even feel when telling my family.

"There's a baby in Stacy's tummy right now," Elizabeth said, and Clara gasped and began running back and forth between the bedroom and living room of our small apartment.

"This is the best day of my life!" she declared.

Minutes later, she sat down and drew us as a family in marker: two oblong blobs with protruding stick arms for Stacy and me, and scribbly blots for both Harrison and Greta. "U R going to be so cute," she wrote. She left it at our apartment, and we put it up on our fridge, underneath the two sonograms of our children, their profiles facing each other and nearly identical.

✧

Stacy is forty-one weeks pregnant. It is 93 degrees, and Harrison seems content inside her belly. At our biometric scan, the doctor assures us everything is fine—his heart rate, her fluid levels, his practice breathing. The placenta is providing him with ample nutrition. "Now you just have to go into labor!" she says brightly, ushering us out.

My parents are visiting; they were supposed to be here to meet Harrison, and instead they find themselves in the company of two miserable adults. We tried to hint to my parents to stay away—the very last thing we want to do in our current miserable limbo is entertain— but my mother steamrolls through our protests with her usual cheery determination. My mother's love is the kind that might leave many things unsaid, but nothing undone.

"I'm sorry if you didn't want us here, Jay," she tells me later, in a quiet moment. "I heard what you were telling me. I just . . . had to be here for you guys. I was feeling pretty powerless. I hope we're helping."

Instead of answering, I take her hand, and I sense it again: our old closeness, or at least its proximate, mournful outline. "You've got to cut that umbilical cord, Mom," John used to say to her, acidly. And so we did. And thank god—what would have become of her otherwise when my first child died? Surely it would have killed her, too. This constant, nagging, polite loneliness in its place: It was a small price to pay in return, wasn't it?

In truth, my parents do help; they offer welcome distraction. My mother walks with the two of us to yoga, and we meet up with one of Stacy's favorite teachers in front of the studio.

"Still?" Michelle asks in disbelief, laughing a little in sympathy. "Oh, guys. He's really taking his time, huh?"

"He **really** likes it in there," Stacy says ruefully.

"Well, are you having sex?" Michelle demands. "You've got to keep at it!" At this, to my amazement, she mimes a ramming motion with her fist.

My mom laughs. "I was going to ask them. But, you know."

"We've been doing that," I deadpan. "And thanks, Michelle. This is my mom, by the way."

"Talk to that baby and tell him you're ready when he is," our doula advises later that day. She's leaving town on the thirty-first, twelve days after our due date, and the way things are going, we begin to wonder if she will even attend the birth. "Maybe investigate if there's something that's been left undone that needs tending to so you can both exhale and feel more ready. Are you in a fight with someone? Is there a project still hanging over your head? Is there a fear or resentment with someone that you need to get off your chest?"

Stacy and I pause at this.

We have arrived at a sort of peace with Greta's spirit. Stacy brought the dove wings home from Golden Willow and had them fashioned into a prayer stick, attached to a piece of deer bone and decorated with crystals—fake diamonds for Greta's birth month and emeralds for the month of her death. We keep it in our living room on a shelf with her picture, a constant reminder of the realms we've passed through on our search for her.

Meanwhile, Greta's ashes remain in our bedroom closet, still in that zippered red canvas bag given to us by the funeral home. They are freighted with meaning, and yet it is hard for us to know what to do with them exactly, or what to feel. Stacy peeked into the sack the night we retrieved them, breaking down sobbing while I stood stone-faced in the doorway. I have never laid eyes on them.

Elizabeth's mother, a sculptor, has made us a hand-thrown urn, a shapely cream-colored vase with a pigeon, her specialty, perched on top of the lid: a city bird, just like Stacy's sparrow. It is immaculate and beautiful, but we have found ourselves unable to conscript it to its designed purpose. We have grown used to the bag in the corner, somehow, a final piece of her that we are both unwilling to face and unwilling to part with.

Now that we are emerging from the underworld, we find ourselves confronted once again by a world full of bodies—meat, sinew, blood. Bodies passing through other bodies, bodies broken and cared for, bodies burned and buried.

It occurs to us now this is the last piece of unfinished business of Greta's death. She needs a resting place before Harrison arrives.

That night, we face the ashes. We both get dressed up; this is a ceremony, after all, and we want to greet it formally. I put on some quiet music, then I turn it off. It doesn't feel right. We stand facing each other, dressed as if for a date night around our living room table. Then we fetch the bag. Unzipping it feels like cracking open a crypt; this bag has been holding shut some of the only remaining secrets of Greta's death. Some part of me is shocked to find the stuffed dog, the muslin blanket from the hospital. I pick up the blanket and set it aside carefully, aware of its few brown spots of blood. I feel their existence without seeing them.

There is a clear plastic sack in here, sealed tight. The bottom of it bulges with weight. I do not want my trembling hands to hold this bag, to tear a hole in its corner, to tip forth its unsteady contents. Stacy, calm and sure, snips the edge with a pair of kitchen shears, exposing what is inside to air.

I have placed a cheap plastic funnel atop her urn, and I stand ready with it. I bought the funnel months ago, for a few dollars, at a kitchen store, for this purpose. I had to ask the woman at the front desk where they were kept. Stacy tips the bag, and the grey ash begins to stream out in wisps. I watch the little bone chips go down. Some of the slightly bigger pieces get stuck. I shake the funnel. We have to turn our heads away to keep from inhaling too much of her. We reserve some of her for our mothers, who have their own empty urns, and zip the bag up. Stacy picks up the urn, now heavier, and sets it on the table, testing it.

It does not rest completely flat. It wobbles, barely perceptibly. It lists. Stacy's face reddens and her crying opens up into wailing, finally. For her, it is not the fact of the ashes' existence that sends her over the edge; that is an awful, awesome fact, so large it cannot be measured. Faced with the unknowable, there is comfort, there is mystery; there can even be meaning. However, the slight unsteadiness of the urn is hurtful, all the way to the very core, just another reminder that the world itself is pitifully inadequate.

Nonetheless, she carries it to the shelf. She sets it down carefully next to the photo of Greta from the funeral service, behind the dove wings. We stand for a moment. Once on the shelf, the urn stands steady, beautiful once more. I look at Stacy's face, which is somehow flushed and drained at the same moment.

There it is; we have done yet another visceral, ghastly thing together as a couple. This was our last act of parenting for Greta's body.

We cry hard; we sob on the couch. I clutch at my head with angry, helpless, balled-up fists. Then we clean up, wash our faces, and behold ourselves in the mirror. Our eyes are blotchy, but otherwise we look unchanged. The act of grieving our daughter continues on, and on, and on. We have held our firstborn child's corpse in our arms, and now there is no limit to what we can endure.

✧

When it finally begins—at twelve p.m. on a Thursday, twelve days after Harrison's due date—it is not exalted. There is no subtle pressure, no slowly widening eyes. We do not clasp hands and inhale deeply together. When it finally begins, it is with a shot of castor oil mixed with orange juice. The oil is our midwife's reluctant suggestion, who warns us: "We're going to induce that baby one way or the other on Friday, hon. So if you want to have tried absolutely **everything** . . ."

Stacy downs the first dose without incident. I watch her nervously as she tips out a tablespoon with a sickening glug, shaking the Tropicana into a scummy froth. She pinches her nose like a little kid, and I wait.

"That wasn't too horrible," she says after a moment. "Now let's wait an hour. If nothing happens, I'll take the rest."

We have whispered and shouted, we have lain down in dirt before a full moon, danced and knelt, prayed and not prayed, lain awake and slept. Now, we watch television, awaiting the stirring of intestines. I sneak a look at Stacy out of the corner of my eye.

"I don't feel anything," she says finally, so I hit "pause" while she mixes up the rest.

Half an hour later, Stacy's contractions have not begun. We resign ourselves: the castor oil did nothing, and tomorrow there will be an induction. Stacy will not go into labor naturally this time. We will not be delivering our baby in the hospital's birthing center, where I would be able to spend the night in the bed with the two of them. Different baby, different pregnancy. Maybe there will be a

C-section. Maybe we will shell out for one of those private rooms. We tell each other it makes more sense this way; like everything else about this process, we have been relieved of control. One way or another, Harrison will be with us tomorrow.

"I must have intestines of steel," Stacy declares.

"I mean, I'm not surprised, weirdly," I say. "Nothing else worked, so why would this? OK, baby boy, tomorrow it is. One way or another, they're gonna get you—"

"Ooohhhh," Stacy says suddenly, fiercely. She stares at me, and her brow crumples. She stands up and bends over at the waist in the same motion, resting a hand on the couch. She says it again, twice as loud for emphasis: "Oohhhhhh." She hobbles, bent over, to the bathroom, but she stops halfway there, bending farther over and expelling a breath like a blown-out tire. I ask her what she feels, and she reaches a hand over the back of her head to swat at me: **No voices, no talking, not now.** She disappears behind the door.

As I watch it shut, I hear her moan again, in a deeper register. I wait helplessly outside the door for a few minutes, listening to her breathing. "Ohhhhhhh," she says. **I am not ready. Oh my god, somehow we are not ready. How could we have waited until the end of time and not be ready?** Life becomes a blur of viscera; I feel only blood coursing through a network of muscles, hear it thundering in my ears.

Some minutes later, Stacy is on the bed, and the timeline seems entirely backward. **Weren't we already at the hospital last time when she moaned this loudly?** Dimly I recall the subtle progress of Greta's labor, the patient buildup over hours, the contractions arriving in comfortingly spaced fifteen-minute intervals.

This is nothing like that. This is jagged, chaotic, insane. Stacy seems to be drowning. She can barely open her eyes between contractions. **We need to be at the hospital.** The message arrives from my rational brain into the heaving sea of my lower brain and nearly disappears before surfacing again. **We need to be at the hospital.**

Our doula, Marianne, has appeared by our side somehow; apparently I have summoned her. I hear her talking to me. She is telling me there's an Uber waiting outside. I'm standing in the doorway of my bedroom, gazing at the spilled-open contents of our go bag. Stacy is still screaming. "Why can't I catch my breath?" she pleads in a piteous voice, in the tiny merciful crack separating two walloping contractions.

I am in the front seat of the car, which is moving, and I hear myself making some sort of joke to the Uber driver, something about getting more than he bargained for. Marianne speaks in a bright, conversational voice, as if we are all just children en route to a playdate. Stacy is on all fours in the backseat next to her, rocking and moaning. She cannot talk to me, and I am like a bug that hit a window, dazed and uncomprehending. My hand reaches back to touch some part of her, and my fingers graze her flank as we exit the tunnel. She is alone in her body; I am alone in my mind. We are animals again, and within this pinhole moment, it feels as if we have never known each other, have forgotten that the world could even possibly contain the other.

As we exit the tunnel into lower Manhattan, everything doubles up and begins rhyming with itself—we have done this before, the drive to a hospital, the screaming, the urgency. Suddenly I'm near the ripped-open place again, watching the curtain flutter between our world and Greta's. Everything in here is exactly as I remember it—the trees' spring leaves the day after she was born, the same leaves catching my eye the week she died. I can feel the air on my arms and on my cheeks, even sitting shotgun in this Uber. **So this is where you both are.**

The car pulls up to the ER entrance. The three of us, Stacy and the doula and I, hobble to the door, a malfunctioning six-legged organism with a backpack swinging off it. Nurses swarm Stacy and put her down in a wheelchair. I trail behind. My legs are concrete, her voice distant. I send a discordantly calm, clear, rational text message to Elizabeth: "Stacy is in labor, and I have gone into shock."

Sending this message into the universe, I feel a measure of my numbness recede. I notice we are in the birthing center room now; Rita is monitoring Harrison's heartbeat while Stacy bends over the bed. Out of muscle memory, I press down hard with flat palms on the small of her back as the contraction takes hold. Reality reassembles itself, a few shreds at a time. It has been less than two hours since labor began. Stacy's contractions have been less than a minute apart for at least forty-five minutes.

"When's the last time you ate something, love?" Rita asks, fetal heart monitor still in hand, pressed to Stacy. It's an alarming question, and I search her eyes but find I cannot pry them from the monitor screen. Stacy's normal voice immediately reemerges from within her, clear and pinched with worry: "About four hours ago? Why?"

Rita doesn't answer, just kneels down on one knee to reposition the heart monitor. "Doooon't worry," she murmurs absently, pressing harder and gazing more intently.

"Rita?" Stacy lifts her head, her labor suddenly forgotten. Her voice is pleading. "Rita, why . . . ?"

"There he is!" Rita says triumphantly. "We just need to get him moving. His heart rate was lagging." She looks up at me, laughing:

"He was asleep. He just woke up, the little bugger. Thanks for joining us, Harrison!"

Stacy and I laugh weakly, and then a contraction catches her and her voice plunges downward a full octave. Rita and Marianne help her into the bathroom while I follow. **Harry,** I think fondly, and I am surprised to hear the nickname, which I'd assumed I would hate, in my mind. "People will call him Harry" was my principal objection to "Harrison," but now I find this endearment floating easily, naturally, in my mind. **Sleepy Prince Harry. You aren't too impressed by any of this, are you?**

Someone turns on the faucet for the huge tub, which takes forty-five minutes to fill up properly. In the meantime, Stacy and I huddle in the shower. Her legs are shaking, and she is standing barefoot on the tile floor; in the moment, her body seems as wet, denuded, and vulnerable as the baby she's trying to deliver. The contractions have swallowed her again, so we cannot talk; instead, I train a showerhead at her lower back. But I feel that the three of us are together—the four of us, Greta's presence like a breath on my neck. I am standing guard while Stacy disappears beneath the rip in the curtain. Somewhere inside there, a little hand will take hers and lead her back to me. **I love you,** I think at her, a message for later. **I love you. When you resurface, I will be here.**

The contractions blur into one long gasping wail. Stacy is being dragged backward now, and I feel in my stomach again that I am losing her. Everyone is behind there: my son, my daughter, my wife. I am seized by a sudden panic that I will somehow not be able to find them or join them, that the curtain will settle and close without me.

"I need to lie down on the bed!" Stacy cries, her voice cutting through the grey room. We spring into action, lifting and negotiating and coaxing. She crawls onto the bed, crouching instinctively on all fours before shaking her head and flipping, just as instinctively, to her back. I feel the tingle in the air now, just as I did with Greta. Now as then, I clamber up onto the bed, nuzzle my head into Stacy's shoulder as she grips my hair. I close my eyes. As I do, the smell of the gauze from Greta's deathbed comes to me. I see Greta, her skull stapled and broken, her brow sweating saline. She opens her eyes and she winks at me. **It's OK, Daddy,** she whispers. **It's OK.** Harrison descends, Stacy pushes, and all three of us disappear behind the rip, each clinging to the other.

Inside here, the knots in my chest vanish. The pumping gallbladder of hatred I've acquired since Greta's death falls silent. I feel everything hard and intractable in me break up and disappear like something dissolving in solution. I can see for light-years in all directions. I look up, and I'm surprised to see a version of myself wandering up a street near my old apartment. It is—what—eight days after the accident? Five? Three? I do not know, but it was the last time I felt so close to the border of life and death. The memory plays out in front of me at a comfortable distance, and I watch myself with fascination, wondering if this scene has been playing on a loop in here until I could come observe it.

"I'm so sorry, baby girl," I am blubbering. "I have to stay here for a long time. That means—that means I'm going to have to forget you a little, baby girl. It's the only way I can stay here. I'm going to have to let go of you a little bit." The distance closes between the two versions of me and I am back in that day, sidewalk beneath my feet, the wind picking up in the big trees. I lift my face toward the branches and glory in their quiet wildness. "But it will only be for a little while, I promise." I wipe away at my streaming face. "Where you are now, it will only be a moment."

Rita's voice reaches my ears, and the branches release me and begin to dissolve as the scene fades. "Yes, that's the way, you're doing great, Mama, you're doing great. You've got a beautiful baby coming right on down. Push that pressure away. Let him come." Stacy goes silent with each push, bearing down, slackening and gasping, and then going completely taut again. She reaches again for me, and I lean all the way in, our foreheads touching, our lips close. I smell her breath, hot and slightly fruity and filling my nostrils and my mouth. I remember the pile of bloody blankets wadded up and thrown away from beneath us after Greta was born, wailing, and I remember the stray smear of meconium on her leg even as they took her to the cold metal scale to weigh her. Stacy and I are plunging down a chute now, slick with fluid. We cling to each other, two people made into one compound animal and sliding, sliding. **We have waded right into the mess together again, my love,** I think.

"One more big one, Stacy, I think you've got it," Rita says, and then Stacy's scream fills my ears and I hear Rita and Marianne crying out, laughing. Suddenly all three of us hit bottom, the curtain fluttering behind us and Stacy clutching him, a white soapy lather of a boy, all arms and legs and a big, ropy grey umbilical cord. He completely covers Stacy's chest, big and rude and squirming and alive, with matted hair and closed eyes that, as I lie on my side weeping, open slightly to meet mine.

He beholds me: his expression is calm, a little bewildered. There is something liquid and dreamy in his eyes in that moment, and he is completely silent. Stacy cannot see us. In that moment, he is still of the void, smuggled whole from eternity, and in those two seconds

I feel like I am watching consciousness fill his eyes like fluid. In that eternal, silent moment, he makes his decision—a cry works its way up through his waterlogged lungs and burbles out, his face reddening. Stacy clutches him to her chest and weeps. **I am here.**

He screams louder while I crouch, shears in hand, and sever the cord, spattering blood on the hospital sheets. As I watch his face, his senses awaken and are flooded from all angles—blaring lights enter his eyes, harsh and unmuffled noises pierce his ears. Blood pumps into his face and turns it scarlet as he screams around and through the liquid in his system. I lean in, smelling the birth on him and kissing the top of his head. His voice resounds in my skull, and in a low croon, I sing quietly to him, my face resting inches from his.

Finding a new song for Harrison felt like a theological problem, beyond the range of human capacity. Not "Between the Bars"—it had to be something tinged with grief but still hopeful. Something true. Early in the pregnancy, I tried "Here Comes the Sun" ("Little darling, it's been a long cold lonely winter"). When he was overdue and we were waiting, I sang him "Goodbye Yellow Brick Road" ("When are you gonna come down? / When are you going to land?").

I finally settle on "In Spite of Ourselves" by John Prine, a country singer whom both Stacy's parents loved. It's a duet between Prine, who was diagnosed with throat cancer the year before recording the song, and Iris DeMent. He is wry, croaky, and barely tuneful; she sounds like someone's loopy aunt. "In spite of ourselves / We'll end up a'sittin' on a rainbow," the chorus goes. "Against all odds / Honey, we're the big door prize." The last line is the kind of promise that you can't technically keep, more prayer than promise: "There won't be nothin' but big old hearts / Dancin' in our eyes."

As I shakily finish singing it, Harrison's screams quiet into whimpers. His long, aristocratic fingers emerge from beneath the hem of the hospital blanket the doula has placed on him, stretch open to the webbing, and close, slowly, into a fist on top of Stacy's breast. The hill of her breast meets the pudge of his cheeks, swollen with absorbed fluid from his extra time in the womb, pushing his bee-stung lips into an involuntary kiss.

I pick up Harrison, so very stout and solid, and place him directly on my chest, in the exact spot I first placed his sister. The moment carries a comet trail of recognition to it, but he is no ghost. My chest rises and falls with his weight on it. I am whole, I realize, with some astonishment. My heart was ripped straight from my chest and placed glistening on the pavement, and yet somehow it beats inside of me still.

Back in the game, I hear in my head, in a voice I do not recognize: a wry sportscaster's voice, someone who has called a thousand plays and still never seen things quite like this before.

✧

Rita informs us that he had a nuchal cord and a true knot. " 'Nuchal' means it was wrapped around his neck. And this"—she reaches down and lifts the cord, rubbery and pale grey and wet, snaking down around Stacy's leg—"is what a true knot looks like."

I contemplate the pretzel shape, about the size of the palm of my hand, six inches down its length. It's pulled just taut enough for the tubes not to kink, resting in a coil that is one hair's breadth of pressure away from closing off.

"A lot of times, these knots get pulled too tight, and babies don't survive." She looks at us meaningfully. "So this is a miracle baby. I hope you understand that."

Later, much later, I will watch the video of Harrison's birth. I will notice the way that Rita's gloved index finger slips discreetly between his neck and the cord that is strangling him, just as his head emerges, to unwrap it with some effort. Yet one more string pulling him back toward oblivion, loosened at the last second.

✧

The days after we bring him home are a dreamy tangle of bedsheets, diapers, pajamas, creams, ointments—Stacy tends to her wounds and we tend to each other, barely dressed. There is a slight discordance haunting the edges of every movement, déjà vu trembling around every action—**Didn't we do this before?**—but in all other respects we are blissful new parents once again.

We spend days simply watching his rib cage rise and fall, waiting for his eyes to open, for him to notice us: I'd forgotten how much of a newborn's life is spent unconscious. Occasionally one of us rouses slightly to watch him breathe some more, but only for a moment or two.

When he is awake, he is calm and still; the first time we place him belly first on a mat so he can practice lifting his head, he simply lies there, head turned to the side and those foggy eyes staring into the distance. I hold him to my chest, and my body slowly memorizes his smell, hairier and hotter than his sister's but otherwise so similar. I feel his soft weight slowly fill out along my chest and strain my arms.

At night, he is awake and quiet; his little black eyes are open like a parked car's headlights. I am certain he is listening to her.

"Stay close to your sister, Harrison," I whisper. "You will never be closer to her than you are right now."

Since Harrison's birth, I feel Greta everywhere. She comes to me in the petals drifting from trees, which I watch fall slowly, little reminders of passing time. She gazes out at me from his eyes, which have the same soft lines underneath—the same genetic material, slightly different admixture, different timelines along parallel branches of fate.

I see synchronicities in the most mundane activities. Waiting in line at the grocery store, I look at the shelf of diapers. I remember, briefly, when I wasn't buying diapers anymore, because my kid was dead. I remember how it felt to look at them on this shelf then. I think about how it feels to look at them and need them again. My chest compresses and I take some odd, gulping breaths to avoid sobbing in the checkout line.

Raw, unprocessed grief like this startles me whenever I find it, like turning over a rock and finding fresh wet dirt. It's then that I realize, or remember, that there are hundreds of spots like these inside of me. **Children die.**

I've learned this firsthand. The knowledge is hardwired into me now; I only have to close my eyes and peer inside to find the repaved roads, the hazard cones and blocked-off exits, the doors sealed shut to avoid contamination.

At two weeks, Harrison chokes and splutters while nursing and is unable to regain his breath. His back arches, his eyes bulge in panic, his mouth foams. We pound his back, the world swims, and I see Death rearing up, tugging at his sleeve. He regains his breath a moment later. I clutch him, my body numb from the shock. A voice whispers in my mind, **You could still lose everything.** The voice will always be right.

Harrison's eyes turn a shocking chlorine blue at three weeks. He learns to support his heavy head, already tufted by more blond hair than Greta had when she was one. It shoots up in a little arcing fountain from the back of his head, surging from twin pools of cowlick. I remember a nurse pointing to those swirls after he was born, saying it meant he was intelligent. I remember one of Greta's last babysitters telling us, after the funeral, that the blue vein running from her left eye to the bridge of her nose meant that our next child would be a boy.

He finds his voice at a month, grinning at the ceiling fan and making little "egguh" and "gock" sounds, and begins babbling a stream of commentary immediately. His smile gets goofier, and Susan jokes he looks like a Borscht Belt comedian. "I don't know how you call him anything but Harry," she says fondly.

Susan lives a mile from us now. After months of fighting and resisting, she has sold her Upper West Side apartment and moved to Brooklyn. "I knew you guys were never going to come see me there again," she admits to us. "And I didn't want you to come back, either. Now I can be part of Harry's life."

In the beginning, she traces the edges of our lives, tentatively but lovingly. When she holds newborn Harrison, I feel the weight in her heart. She hunches in fear, but her face beams love at him, a signal sent with effort and sheer will.

✧

On her fourth birthday, we stop telling and retelling the same Greta stories. The time she's been gone has begun to eclipse the time she was alive, like an elongating late-afternoon shadow, and revisiting the same well-worn memories feels like sifting through pebbles. Instead, we invite her to join us again in the present. Harrison, now eight months old, sits in the dirt with us in the park, near the ducks she loved to point out to us. I gesture toward a small bird pecking away at wood chips nearby. "You see this birdie?" I ask him. "Sometimes your sister sends those."

We tell him about her, lightly and casually. We want him to know about her, but we haven't figured out the vocabulary yet, so we mention her when the spirit catches us and say a small prayer that we are doing it right. **Your sister loved bananas, too. You have your sister's potty sense of humor. Your sister was a real pain in the ass about sleep.** When he touches a tree, I tell him to say hello to her, and his face softens.

Susan is with us, as are Jack and Lesley. We all remark on what a beautiful day it is.

Harrison sits contently on Jack's lap, and Jack keeps one hand on him while the other holds a can of seltzer. It's been months since he's had a drink.

"Happy fourth birthday, Greta Greene," Stacy says next to me. She has taken the day off from her new job, at the hospital where Greta was born. It's a small piece of serendipity, an invitation to stay connected to her. None of her patients has any idea that Stacy nursed her own child here, a child now gone.

Two years after her death, we have to work to find ways to connect with Greta. What was once a tidal wave of grief has shrunk to a running faucet somewhere in our consciousness, and we need to make dates, occasionally, to grieve her. We seek out plays, movies about death and loss, crying quietly in the theater. There is something bittersweet in this need to remember. During the first year, the year of her death, the emptiness was overpowering, and we constantly sought her out. Now we are being filled by the deafening song of Harrison's ongoing existence. It leaves us haggard and split open and grateful at all times, and with no time for anything further.

Harrison is growing the way a creek floods, imperceptibly and with alarming speed. We love him in specifics now, delight in the way he differs from her. He is warmer than his sister, less intense and less easily perturbed. He is unguarded, more generous with physical affection. Greta ate daintily, delivered spoonfuls of yogurt directly into her mouth without a droplet lost. He eats like a caveman, smearing green stuff all over his high chair and letting out wet burpy giggles through mouthfuls of hummus and guacamole that spatter the table.

Music electrifies him, where it only vaguely interested her. When I play him upbeat tunes with bright voices—the Beatles, say, or Harry Nilsson—he sits up on his haunches and bounces ecstatically.

He is energetic, joyful, and, above all, content. When we go outside, he grins at me like we just got off a late shift somewhere and we have some pocket money. He seems to constantly appreciate something simple about our lives, a fact that never stops dawning on him in real time: we get to spend time together.

Under his tutelage, I can feel a frankly ludicrous conviction growing inside of me. We—myself and my wife, this growing child in front of us and the one we never see—are going to be all right. It's a childlike notion, a delusion, and my body fights it. Moments after the thought flashes clearly across my mind, I recoil. **No,** the deeper voice whispers.

As if in response to this voice, Harrison comes down with seemingly every bug in existence. When he is eight months, we pull him out of his crib sweating, writhing, aflame. His temperature reads 105, and he has no other symptoms. We put him in the tub, watch him shiver, while I call the pediatrician. His fever subsides with medicine, and she tells us to come in the next morning.

"It's just a virus," she tells us. "A nasty one, but it's going around everywhere. Trust me, I've seen it again and again. It freaks the parents out, but it will pass."

When the fever persists on the ninth day, she sends us for blood work. **Of course,** I think. **This is how it will happen. This is the beginning.** His white blood cell count is suspiciously elevated—inconclusive. Grim and wordless, we take him to the very same ER—Weill Cornell, back up FDR Drive. We park in the same lot, walk through the same glass doors. Harrison sits on my hip, waving and smiling and babbling to everyone. I am assailed by the sight of the orange plastic chair Stacy collapsed in, right outside the room where I first saw Greta's lifeless body.

"Have you been here before?" a tattooed woman in triage asks us without looking up.

"Your son has an ear infection," a doctor says three minutes into examining him. "He looks pretty healthy to me. And happy."

"Guh-gock," Harrison responds cheerily. We thank her, carry him out, an antibiotic prescription in our hands, and strap our son back into our car seat and drive him home, the ER receding behind us. I had almost forgotten this place existed, this building that my daughter never left. We have delivered another one of our children into it, and we are leaving it again, intact. We feel stunned, thunderstruck, impossibly grateful.

At nine months, Harrison tumbles down our apartment stairs. He cries hard for a minute, seems groggy for a few seconds, and then is fine. I wait for days, weeks, anticipating in terror signs of brain damage that never appear.

He wakes up crying inconsolably a month later. He screams and screams for hours, unable to calm himself even when nursing. "Something's very wrong!" Stacy wails in the dark of the night. Our guts drop; Death claws at our ankles, hell yawning back open and hungering to swallow us all.

I take him for another appointment the next morning: coxsackie virus, or hand, foot, and mouth disease. Something else Greta never got. He recovers in a few days.

It occurs to us only later what these awful incidents are giving us: scares. Normal, unremarkable, everyday parenthood scares, the kind we were never afforded with Greta. Greta never fell, never broke a bone. With each accident, each illness, Harrison is teaching us: **Sometimes children live.**

We share these bumps in the road with new friends, new parents, who know of our daughter only as something that happened to us. We are entering into the merry-go-round of first parenting with them, and we try to keep ourselves soft, surprised, and wide-eyed at every development: every baby's tantrum, their first teeth, the quirks of their development. We are both new and not new at this, and we tread carefully through the twin shocks of discovery and déjà vu.

As time passes, Greta's toys begin to shed some of their personal meaning. Harrison carries around Daisy, the stuffed dog that had accompanied her at the hospital, everywhere now. Our old high chair was caked with bits of Greta's food; it seemed only practical to scrub those food bits off and sit him down in it. We give him all her old cups and bowls, but somewhere on the top shelf one remains, a sippy cup with her name on masking tape from her daycare. Her pink scooter sits in the back of the closet still, waiting for Harrison when he is ready for it. Greta never was.

Susan devotes herself to him: "How's my Harry?" she cries when I bring him over to her building, as he wiggles and strains and attempts to melt himself out of his stroller straps, his supplicating hands stretching up, desperate to be received. "There's my baby genius," she says, scooping him up as he lays his head on her shoulder.

"He's a **genius**," she insists to me, fixing me with a meaningful stare. "The other day I asked him which pillow he wanted to nap on, this one or that one. He said, 'That one,' clear as day."

"Amazing," I say, smiling a little. Harrison has said a number of words so far that it seems only Grandma Suz can hear.

Susan's new building is big and airy and anonymous, with a massive third-floor office complex. Harrison likes to play on the couches there. He likes to throw her reading glasses on the floor and laugh. There is a playroom full of toys, pumping nonstop pop music, that they have nearly to themselves, since the building is at half capacity. She follows him around as he scoops up her valuables and tosses them into corners. "I am perfectly content to be Harry's servant," she declares when I ask her if he is too much.

The two of them almost never go outside, however. Susan can't quite bear to contemplate it yet. One day out walking alone, something in the air catches her eye—a movement of shadow, a bird maybe. For a half second, she imagines a foreign object plummeting from above. Her new doorman doesn't understand why she is sobbing as she stumbles blindly back inside. She spends the next day and a half in bed, inundated by flashbacks.

In this way, the uneasy music of our lives plays on, mingling dread and love, fear and bliss. We have long wondered what became of the families that received Greta's organs. Wouldn't the boy with her heart be about five years old now? What about the two men sharing her kidneys, the girl with her liver? For the first time since leaving the hospital, we contact LiveOnNY to find out the fate of the recipients.

One of the grown men who received a kidney is no longer following up for treatment. They have no status update on his health. "Well, I don't feel great about **that**," Stacy says. I grimace. Neither of us voices the awful unspoken thing we are feeling—**We gave you a piece of our daughter's body. The least you could do is take care of it**—because it is too ugly for us, too insane. But each of us hears the other thinking it.

The boy who received Greta's heart did not survive. He died a year after the transplant, a year he spent hospitalized. Stacy's eyes go lifeless at the news. For the first time in months, I walk in search of an unpopulated corner, rage burbling its way up my throat. At the end of our block, I scream at the empty shipping containers near the pier. It's another infuriating reminder: her body is no longer ours to save, ours to protect.

Bouts of blinding anger like this still overwhelm me occasionally. I am usually somewhere public when they happen, smiling as they detonate. I am learning to accept them, to live with this endless cycle of remission and metastasis. **I am allowed to be angry forever.** I tell this to myself again and again. **I am allowed to be confused forever.** I had a child die and chose to become a father again. There can be no greater definition of stupidity or bravery, insanity or clarity, hubris or grace. In my moments of strength, I simply surrender to this confusion and allow it to envelop me.

In moments of serenity I find myself back in the big open field, the one from my vision at Golden Willow. I am both buried in the ground and standing on it, gazing up at a vast open sky. Here the stars stretch endlessly, looming above like prehistoric creatures. The longer I stare at them, the more I hear the voices of both of my children. They stand beside me—Harrison at my left, Greta at my right. We gaze up at them together. In this exalted place, they both hear me, and I can say to them what needs saying.

Harrison, baby boy. We must learn to balance something very tricky—you, me, your mother, and your sister. I do not know how to teach you. You have to learn to know your sister and also to be at peace with her absence. We are still here, and we must learn to embrace our fragile lives.

The world points you away from these questions, Harrison, not toward them. It pulls you like a stone to the bottom of the ocean. We must learn to float between, everything visible above and below. Daddy is still learning how. I want you to live with this knowledge inside of you. Maybe I can watch and learn it, secretly, from you.

I feared, when you were delivered into

our hands, that we were going to damage
you. My wounds are still healing, but a dead
corner of my heart remains. I wonder: Do
you see that dead corner, too? Do you fear it?

I am slowly learning that you see everything I endeavor to hide from you, and that
you are unafraid. Your eyes are clearer than
mine, and your heart sturdier. I suspect you
will understand more of what you see in me
than I ever will.

I have had a vision since you were born,
Harrison. Your mommy and I were in this
big field together, crouched down at the base
of a tree. I reached down to rest my fingers
on the moss, pliant and damp. I pressed my
palm to it, and your mommy laid her hand
on top of mine. Together, our hands sank,
and we lay down together in the mud. I saw
an old man walk up to us. His eyes were
slightly watery and blue, creased with kindness. His skin was spotted, his hair a little
yellowed. He stood above us, a little sad but
contented, and looked down at us. He had
your eyes, baby boy. Thank you. Thank you
for letting us come here first.

Greta, baby girl: Are you near? I think that when I feel you, it is your empathy that I feel: your belief that everyone deserved and needed peace, and that you were a first responder to help bring it. I admired that so much about you, Greta—you had a beautiful soul, and you had room in it for everyone.

I still have a long time before we find each other again, Greta, and I am sure I will yearn for you during much of that time. But here's one thing I know, and I think I have you to thank for it: I know you do not struggle. I can sense that you are at peace, with both yourself and your time with us. I can sense you stepping in, where you see an opening, to direct us through our path. When I stick my hands in dirt, I hear you giggle and whisper to me.

Stay close to Harrison, OK? There are many things about his life that only you can teach him. He needs you. And I know you are a very old spirit by now, but please—stay close to me. I need you, too, and I will look for you wherever I go.

Harrison, this is where she lives in me.

Do you see her, too? Come closer. I want us to walk out of this field together, but first let's wait one moment more.

Do you see the sky? Do you feel the cool air? It's wonderful, isn't it?

Are we ready?

Take my hands, guys.

OK, let's go.

ACKNOWLEDGMENTS

Even in our darkest times, Stacy and I were held aloft by too many to count. It would be impossible to thank everyone by name, but every single act of kindness sent our way, no matter how small, sustained us.

Profound thanks to my agent, Anna Sproul-Latimer, for the ferocity of her belief and for the personal connection she forged with Greta through these pages. Thank you to Howard Yoon and Gail Ross for shaping the book in its earliest stages. Thank you to everyone at Knopf—especially my editor, Jordan Pavlin, who treated both me and this material with extraordinary sensitivity, kindness, and care. I am forever grateful.

My Pitchfork family cared for me and gave me purpose at a time of great need. Special thanks to Mark Richardson, Ryan Schreiber, and Chris Kaskie for allowing me space to grieve. For advice, encouragement, support, presence, and friendship, at Pitchfork and beyond: Stacey Anderson, Ryan Dombal, Corban Goble, Lindsay Hood, Jessica Hopper, Joe Keyes, Claire Lobenfeld, Kevin Lozano, Jill Mapes, Quinn Moreland, Puja Patel, Jenn Pelly, Amanda Petrusich, Amy Phillips, Matthew Schnipper, Brandon Stosuy, Lindsay Zoladz, and Charlotte Zoller.

Thank you to our Ditmas parent community, Greta's friends and loved ones, who brought us hot food, sheltered us, cried with us, and never once flinched. Special thanks to Jenna and Brock, to Jeff and Sam, to Amanda and Aaron, to Jen and Lev. Thank you to everyone at Michelle St. Claire daycare, who Greta loved deeply. She flourished immeasurably in your care.

Thank you to the Upper West Side community for the love and support you provided Susan.

Thanks to Liz and Anna, sisters to us in all but name, for seeing us through the worst, for working tirelessly even in deep grief to honor Greta's life. To Andrew and Andy, who supported them and us in turn. Thank you to Helane Anderson for the spiritual guidance.

Thank you to Danny and Elizabeth—our friends, our family, and our first responders forever. Thank you to Vicky Gold, for Greta's beautiful hand-thrown urn; to Clara, for keeping Greta's memory alive and for her devotion to Harrison; to Caitlin Hurd for our beautiful painting of Greta. To Chris and Randy, for offering us a home between homes.

To Nils Bernstein, who rallied hundreds for a fund to plant a tree in Prospect Park bearing Greta's name, and to everyone who contributed. More than $19,000 was donated to the PICU at Weill-Cornell in Greta's name, and we are grateful to everyone who made that possible. Special thanks to Ben and Giorgia for setting up a GoFundMe in our names and for everyone who gave.

Thanks to William LoTurco and Kate Mack, for encouraging me to go down this path in the first place, and to Nancy Rawlinson for her crucial feedback. Thanks to Maris Kreizman for believing in me early and always making time.

Thank you to David Kessler and team, for generosity of time and of spirit. Thank you to everyone at Golden Willow, and thank you to Tom Hart and Leela Corman, for the inspiration.

Thanks to all our yoga teachers—Martha, Mimi, Michelle, Liz, and everyone at Third Root.

Thank you to all fellow grieving parents who provided solace and inspiration. Special thanks to Jo and Bill and the memory of their beautiful son Jack.

Thank you to our family. To John, Melissa, Nik, and Ana; to my mother, who told me I should consider writing a book. To my father, who taught me what selfless devotion looks like. To Susan, Jack, and Lesley, who trusted me with their story and offered their unconditional love. To Diane, for her eagle-eyed proofreading.

But most and above all, thank you, Stacy. You watched over this book carefully and made sure it was true. This is your story, too, and I am honored that you trusted in me to tell it. Words can never do justice to the wife, mother, and partner that you are. With your innate wisdom, your emotional intelligence, and your capacity for empathy and love, you are my compass in the world, forever and always.

A Note About the Author

JAYSON GREENE is a contributing writer and former senior editor at Pitchfork. His writing has appeared in **The New York Times**, Vulture, and **GQ**, among other publications. This is his first book. He lives in Brooklyn with his wife and son.